LONGMAN

INSIGHTS *into* BUSINESS

MICHAEL LANNON

GRAHAM TULLIS

TONYA TRAPPE

Contents

	PRE-READING	TEXT	LANGUAGE FOCUS	SKILLS FOCUS
UNIT 1 COMPANY STRUCTURES	Listening – The departments of an organisation 3M Corporate Organisation Chart	READING – '3M: An American Star in Europe' (*Eurobusiness*)	Present perfect and Past simple Describing changes in quantities (increase and decrease)	LISTENING – Describing responsibilities within a company: Manley Johnson, 3M France SPEAKING – Presenting companies WRITING – Company profiles
UNIT 2 RECRUITMENT	Matching job advertisements with covering letters	READING – 'Looks: appearance counts with many managers' (*International Herald Tribune*)	Present simple and Present continuous	READING – Studying job advertisements WRITING – Preparing a CV and letter of application LISTENING – Selecting candidates and job interviews – David Smyth, Europe Assistance SPEAKING – Role play of an interview
UNIT 3 MANAGEMENT STYLES	Management styles in five different countries	READING – 'Be nice and smile if you want to hire a Hungarian manager' (*The European*)	Adjectives of nationality Expressing fractions and proportions	LISTENING – Tom Scheck talks about the problems involved in international negotiations SPEAKING – Cultural differences – Role play: Giving and asking for advice
UNIT 4 ADVERTISING AND MARKETING	Advertising media Product endorsements Advertising slogans	READING – 'In Ads, US Stars Shine For Japanese Eyes Only' (*Washington Post*)	Gerund and Infinitive	SPEAKING – Describing target markets; Analysing advertisements LISTENING – Customer profiles and marketing strategy: Manfred Kozlowsky, Harley-Davidson
UNIT 5 FRANCHISING	Categories of franchises Listening – Tony Dutfield of the British Franchise Association	READING – 'Small slice of the Big Action' (*The European*)	Relative clauses	LISTENING – Three executives discuss franchisor/franchisee relations – Interview with Peter Stern, senior franchise manager for the National Westminster Bank SPEAKING – Taking out a franchise with Budget Rent a Car and Perfect Pizza WRITING – Report on UK franchise market
UNIT 6 JAPAN AND THE BUSINESS WORLD	The performance of Japanese business Comparison of hours worked in different countries	READING – 'Dying to work' (*US News and World Report*)	Expressing contrast	WRITING – The memo LISTENING – Tips for doing business in Japan: Tomomi Moriwake
UNIT 7 BUSINESS AND THE ENVIRONMENT	Environmental cartoons The role of business in environmental affairs	READING – 'A banner of values' (*Inc.*)	The Passive Describing groups and subgroups	SPEAKING – Environmental case studies; Labels and packaging LISTENING – A Body Shop customer survey; The role of companies and environmental affairs: David Wheeler, The Body Shop WRITING – Are your purchasing decisions based on environmental concerns?

	PRE-READING	TEXT	LANGUAGE FOCUS	SKILLS FOCUS
UNIT 8 **RETAILING**	Retailing in the UK and in continental Europe Listening – Dr Steve Burt, Stirling University	READING – 'Richer pickings' *(Business)*	Make or do Locating objects	LISTENING – Store layouts SPEAKING/WRITING – Consumer buying habits
UNIT 9 **BANKING**	Listening – Peter Milson, Midland Bank Banking items and documents	READING – 'Hobs' Home and Office Banking System *(Bank of Scotland brochure)*	Allow/enable/let First and second conditional	SPEAKING – Making and answering enquiries about bank documents LISTENING – Alain Depussé, French businessman: a company and its banks WRITING – A letter of complaint to a bank
UNIT 10 **THE STOCK EXCHANGE**	Headlines from the financial pages – Assessing the performance of listed companies' shares	READING – 'The Stock Exchange' *(Banking Information Service)*	Third conditional	READING – Studying share price listings LISTENING – European stock market turnovers. Characteristics of stock exchanges: Stuart Valentine of the London Stock Exchange WRITING – Summarising the evolution of a company's share prices
UNIT 11 **CORPORATE ALLIANCES AND ACQUISITIONS**	Extracts from the financial press	READING – 'Getting Together' *(Time)*	Reported speech	SPEAKING – Describing technical data and performance of cars LISTENING – The Renault/Volvo alliance – Margareta Galfard, Volvo, France WRITING – Memo recommending a course of action
UNIT 12 **THE SMALL BUSINESS**	Advantages and disadvantages of small business Listening – Checklist for starting a business: Ben Fox of Fasta Pasta	READING – 'Deliver us from debt' *(Financial Times)*	Could have + past participle Should have + past participle	LISTENING – Advice for starting a business: Ben Fox, Fasta Pasta SPEAKING – Small business questionnaire WRITING – Business plan
UNIT 13 **INTERNATIONAL TRADE**	Listening – Why countries trade OECD Economist Europe quiz	READING – 'A Spanish Oracle' *(Super Marketing)*	Modal verbs of obligation Describing trends	WRITING – Describing the evolution of wool prices from a graph LISTENING – An economist from the OECD speaks about protectionism and the European Community's Common Agricultural Policy SPEAKING – Completing a graph
UNIT 14 **INSURANCE**	Listening – Identifying types of risk	READING – 'Insurance Services' *(Corporation of London brochure)*	Expressing approximation	LISTENING – Don Raley, insurance expert, talks about Lloyds SPEAKING – Evaluating risk WRITING – Report on evaluation of risk forms
UNIT 15 **CORPORATE IDENTITY**	Analysing a BP corporate advertisement	READING – 'How the decisions were made' *(An Image for the 90s – from a BP publication)*	The Article	LISTENING – Glen Tuttsel of the Michael Peters' design consultancy talks about logos, design and corporate identity SPEAKING – Convincing a sponsor WRITING – Request letter

Company Structures

KEY VOCABULARY

Most companies are made up of three groups of people: the **shareholders** (who provide the capital), the **management**, and the **workforce**. The management structure of a typical company is shown in the following **organisation chart**:

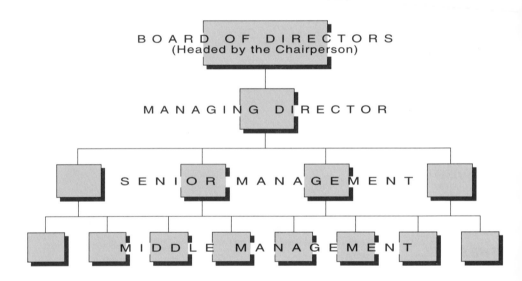

BOARD OF DIRECTORS
(Headed by the Chairperson)

MANAGING DIRECTOR

SENIOR MANAGEMENT

MIDDLE MANAGEMENT

At the top of the company hierarchy is the **Board of Directors**, headed by the **Chairperson** (or **President**). The Board is responsible for making policy decisions and for determining the company's strategy. It will usually appoint a **Managing Director** (or **Chief Executive Officer**) who has overall responsibility for the running of the business. **Senior managers** head the various departments or functions within a company, which may include the following:

Marketing	**Public Relations**	**Personnel** (or **Human Resources**)
Finance	**Production**	**Research and Development**

LEAD-IN

1 You will hear six people talking about their work. Listen and decide which of the six departments listed above they work for.

1 ....   4 ....

2 ....   5 ....

3 ....   6 ....

2 3M is a major multinational company which manufactures more than 60,000 different products. In groups, study the 3M organisation chart which shows just some of the company's main activities, then decide which department or sector is responsible for each of the following:

1 Reflective material for motorways and street signs
2 Scanners, colour print film and projection equipment
3 Aerosol products for people suffering from asthma
4 Decisions concerning salaries and benefits of employees
5 Scotch Magic Tape and Post-it Notes
6 3M United Kingdom
7 Computer Diskettes

3M Corporate Organisation Chart

L.D. De Simone
Chairman and Chief
Executive Officer

DEPARTMENTS

Engineering, Quality and Manufacturing Services	Finance	Human Resources	Legal Affairs	Research and Development	Corporate Secretary

SECTORS

R.A. Mitsch
Executive Vice President, Industrial and Consumer Sector

• Industrial tape
• Automotive systems
• Commercial office supply
• Consumer stationery
• Abrasive technologies
• Special adhesives and chemicals

L.E. Eaton
Executive Vice President, Information, Imaging and Electronic Sector

• Printing and publishing systems
• Photo colour systems
• Telecom systems
• Electrical products
• Consumer and professional video and audio technology
• Data storage diskette and optical technology

J.E. Robertson
Executive Vice President, Life Sciences Sector

• Medical products
• Healthcare services
• Dental products
• Traffic and personal safety products
• Traffic control materials

H.A. Hammerly
Executive Vice President, International Operations

• Europe
• Asia Pacific
• Canada
• Latin America and Africa

November 1, 1992

Company profile

3M: AN AMERICAN STAR IN EUROPE

TIM HINDLE

3M is the epitome of all that is best in
corporate America. To stay on top the company must
export its virtues to Europe.

The far-reaching fruits of innovation

Whenever lists of America's brightest and best are compiled 3M is guaranteed to feature.

3M was born early this century as Minnesota Mining & Manufacturing. The mining soon ceased when the company's founders failed to dig up the corundum they had hoped to discover. So they turned to trading in sandpaper, a product that uses the abrasive corundum. From the beginning the company was forced to innovate or die.

Today 3M's headquarters and many of its laboratories are in St Paul, Minnesota. Most of its customers are other industrial concerns. Its 60,000 products range from medical-imaging equipment to Scotch tape to abrasives for the car industry. With that unpromising background, how has the company been so successful?

Perpetual innovation
When asked to explain its own success, 3M begins with technological innovation.

3M is among the 25 companies with the most patents in the world – 11 of the 25 are Japanese, 10 are American and only four are European. The company spends some 6.5% of its total sales on research and development, almost twice the American average. And that has increased from about 4.5% at the beginning of the 1980s. The increase – part of the response to the less sparkling performance in the mid-1980s – adds a not-insignificant $200 million a year to the research budget.

European action
3M sees its future as lying increasingly outside the United States. Europe accounts for some 30% of the company's worldwide sales and one-quarter of its employees. That puts 3M among the 300 largest companies in Europe.

The company has had subsidiaries in the region for almost 40 years and now has 17 different companies on the continent and 14 major R&D centres. Since 1984 a number of European Management Action Teams (EMATs) have been set up under the direction of Joe Warren, 3M's Brussels-based vice-president in charge of Europe.

Briefly, 3M worldwide is divided into four sectors: industrial and electronics (36% of sales); information and imaging technologies (28%); life sciences (22%); and commercial and consumer (14%). These four sectors are divided into 15 "strategic business centres" (SBCs) – for audio-visual products, abrasives, etc. – and each centre is responsible for three or four of the company's 50 operating divisions. The operating divisions are run like small businesses and 3M staff say that each has its own culture.

Global strategy is determined by the business centres in St Paul. European input comes via group directors (one for each business centre) based at 3M's European headquarters in Brussels. In addition, the European organisation has a number of product managers (most of them in Brussels) plus managing directors in charge of each of the 17 European subsidiaries. These subsidiaries are run nationally, with a few exceptions – for example, the MD of Spain is also the MD of Portugal, and the MD of the UK is also MD of Ireland.

Each of the 40-plus EMATs corresponds roughly to an operating division and has between eight and ten members drawn from different functions and different countries. Typically they meet every four to six weeks. In theory they have collective responsibility for achieving the company's European goals; in practice they spend much of their time discussing the launch of new products.

Although 3M has only 150 Americans working for the company outside the United States (even in the UK there are only six American employees), the language of the EMATs is English. Since these were the first formal means for more junior employees of different nationalities to get together, the early discussions tended to be dominated by the fluent English-speakers: the British, the Dutch and the Irish. Now the company insists that a certain level of proficiency in English is a prerequisite for joining an EMAT, and team members are being trained to learn how to accommodate different cultures.

The future depends on how well the company has learnt to adapt to change. One of the greatest changes in its markets is occurring in Europe, and much hangs on the ability of the EMATs to come up with products that will meet the fast-shifting demands of 3M's European customers.

Eurobusiness

READING

1 Read the text on the opposite page and answer the following questions.

1 How did 3M get its name?

2 How has 3M managed to become such a successful company?

3 What role do the EMATs play in 3M's European organisation?

4 What does 3M's future in Europe depend on?

2 Scan the text quickly and find the figures, percentages or sums of money that correspond to the following pieces of information.

Example: The number of 3M products   *60,000*
....

1 The sum of money added to 3M's research budget every year   ....

2 The number of 3M subsidiaries in Europe   ....

3 The number of major 3M research and development centres in Europe   ....

4 The number of strategic business centres   ....

5 The percentage of total sales of 3M's industrial and electronics sector   ....

6 The percentage of total sales which 3M spends on R&D   ....

7 The number of Americans working for 3M outside the USA   ....

8 The percentage of total sales of 3M in Europe   ....

Practise reading the figures aloud, then listen to the cassette and check your pronunciation.

3 Now listen and write down the numbers you hear.

1 ....   **5** ....

2 ....   **6** ....

3 ....   **7** ....

4 ....   **8** ....

VOCABULARY

1 Match the words from the text with their corresponding definitions.

1 trade (*line 9*)   **a** work done in order to make new discoveries

2 innovate (*line 12*)   **b** results obtained over a period of time

3 concern (*line 16*)   **c** to do business; to buy and sell

4 patent (*line 25*)   **d** amount of money used for a specific purpose

5 research (*line 29*)   **e** to make changes and introduce new ideas

6 increase (*line 31*)   **f** to go up; to rise

7 performance (*line 34*)   **g** a company or business

8 budget (*line 36*)   **h** a legal document which gives a person or company the exclusive right to make or sell an invention

2 Some of the words in the following sentences are in bold. Look through lines 44 to 112 of the text and identify the words that were actually used to express the same ideas.

1 3M has had its own **local companies** in Europe for 40 years.
2 Joe Warren is **responsible for** European business. He has helped **establish** several EMATs since 1984.
3 There are four main **divisions** in which 3M does business worldwide.
4 The operating divisions are **managed** like small businesses and, according to **employees**, each division has its own culture.
5 The company's **plan of action** is determined in St Paul.
6 The **central offices** of 3M Europe are located in Brussels.
7 The EMATs are responsible for **reaching** the company's European **objectives**.
8 The EMATs often discuss the **introduction** of new products onto the market.
9 In the future, the EMATs will have to **think of** products that will meet the demands of European customers.

3 Complete the following passage using words from the left-hand column of exercise 1 and words that you found in exercise 2.

Since the beginning of the century, 3M has known that it must continually
[1]............................ in order to survive. Indeed, the company has been responsible for the [2]............................ of 60,000 products, each of which is protected by a [3]............................

The successful [4]............................ of 3M over the years is due to several factors. Firstly, the company spends a large part of its annual [5]............................ on the creation, improvement and testing of products. The company also has a flexible structure which allows employees to change jobs frequently, from [6]............................ to manufacturing, or from manufacturing to marketing. The exchange of ideas and information is also a key aspect of 3M's [7]............................ of constant innovation. Top technical people attend an annual meeting at the [8]............................ in St Paul where many 3M laboratories show their latest products. Another interesting fact about 3M is that it encourages [9]............................ to spend 15% of their time on personal projects. It was this unusual policy which enabled 3M employee Arthur Fry to [10]............................ one of the most famous 3M inventions – the Post-it note.

DISCUSSION

Read the following description of how 3M developed its famous Post-it notes.

Spencer Silver was a 3M research chemist whose objective was to produce the strongest adhesive on the market. Although he did not succeed in his mission, he did develop another type of adhesive that had two interesting properties: it could be re-used and it left no residue on the material to which it was applied. However, no one at 3M could find a use for this product and it was put aside temporarily.

Ten years later, one of Silver's colleagues, Art Fry, discovered a new use for the abandoned adhesive. Fry sang in a choir and used strips of paper to mark the pages of his hymn book, which fell out every time he opened the book. He therefore decided to apply Silver's adhesive to the strips and found that they marked the pages and did not fall out when the book was opened. This was the first step in the discovery of the future Post-it note.

1 Why do you think this product has become so popular?
2 The Post-it notes were invented thanks to the fact that 3M allows employees to spend 15% of their time working on personal projects. Do you think this idea could be extended to other types of companies?

LANGUAGE FOCUS

PRESENT PERFECT AND PAST SIMPLE

Look at the following sentences from the text:

*The mining soon **ceased** when the company's founders **failed** to dig up the corundum they had hoped to discover.* (line 6)
*The company **has had** subsidiaries in the region for almost 40 years.* (line 44)

■ Which tense is used in (a) the first sentence, and (b) the second sentence?
■ Which tense has a connection with the present? Which tense only tells us about the past?

➤➤ For more information on the present perfect and past simple, turn to page 153.

Practice

Complete the following company profile with either the present perfect or past simple tense of the verbs in brackets. You should pay particular attention to irregular verbs and to the position of adverbs.

 COLGATE-PALMOLIVE COMPANY

William Colgate [1].................................. (found) the Colgate Company in 1806 as a starch, soap and candle business in New York City. For the first one hundred years, the company [2]................................. (do) all its business in the United States. However, in the early 1900s, the company [3]................................. (begin) an aggressive expansion programme that [4]................................. (lead) to the establishment of Colgate operations in countries throughout Europe, Latin America and the Far East. Recently it [5]................................. (set up) operations in Turkey, Pakistan, Saudi Arabia, Eastern Europe and China. Colgate-Palmolive [6]................................. (become) a truly global consumer products company, worth $6.6 billion and selling in more than 160 countries.

Colgate-Palmolive's five main sectors of business are: Oral Care, Body Care, Household Surface Care, Fabric Care and Pet Nutrition and Health Care. In the area of Oral Care, Colgate-Palmolive is the world leader in toothpaste. Since 1980, the company [7]................................. (increase) its share of this market by more than 12% to over 40% today. Oral care revenues [8]................................. (grow) significantly in recent years and in 1991, they [9]................................. (exceed) $1.3 billion. As a result of the company's heavy investment in research and technology, it [10]................................. (develop) many successful toothpastes, rinses and toothbrushes. To strengthen its presence in professional products, Colgate-Palmolive [11]................................. (buy) the Ora Pharm Company of Australia and the dental therapeutics business of Scherer Laboratories USA in 1990. For many years, the company [12]................................. (have) a strong dental

education programme in schools throughout the world and [13]................................. (maintain) a close partnership with the international dental community. Recently Colgate-Palmolive [14]................................. (enlarge) its school education programmes to cover rural areas as well as townships in developing countries. For the last three years, the company [15]................................. (be) a major sponsor of the International Dental Congress, the world's largest and most prestigious dental meeting.

The company [16]................................. (always pay) close attention to the environment. It [17]................................. (already make) great progress in the use of recyclable bottles and packaging materials. In 1990 the American Council on Economic Priorities [18]................................. (choose) Colgate-Palmolive as one of the four most socially responsible companies in the United States.

DESCRIBING CHANGES

The following verbs can be used to describe upward (↗) and downward (↘) movements in price, quantity and amount:

Intransitive verbs (verbs which do not have an object)			**Transitive verbs** (verbs which have an object)		
↗ increase	rise	go up	↗ increase	raise	
↘ decrease go down	fall decline	drop	↘ decrease	reduce	drop

The population of the world is increasing.
The prices of electronic goods have fallen.

The government has increased income tax.
We have reduced our prices by 10 per cent.

The following nouns can also be used:

↗ an increase	a rise			
↘ a decrease	a fall	a drop	a decline	a reduction

Practice

Complete the following sentences using a noun or a verb from the list above. Do not use the same word more than once.

1 As a result of the recession, we have had to .... the amount of money we spend on research and development.

2 Last year was a good year for the company and our sales .... considerably.

3 The price of coffee has .... as a result of bad weather conditions.

4 Many Asian companies have entered the market and there has been a 20% .... in prices.

5 Some governments fear the .... in Japanese investment in Europe.

6 The .... in profits is the result of poor management.

SKILLS FOCUS

LISTENING

1 Before you listen to the cassette, study the following structures which are used to describe a person's responsibilities within a company and to show his or her position in the company hierarchy. The sentences refer to the 3M organisation chart on page 5.

A *Who* | *is* | *in charge of* | *the Life Sciences sector?*
                   | *responsible for* |
         | *heads* |

B *J. E. Robertson.*

A *Who* | *does he* | *report to* | *?*
                 | *work under* |
         | *is he responsible to* | *.*

B *L. D. De Simone.*

2 You will hear a speaker describing some of the different positions that Mr Manley Johnson, a senior manager of 3M, held throughout his professional life until 1989. Listen and complete the table on the following page.

Division or sector	No. of years in position	Name of superior	Responsibilities
	—	—	*Worked on improving many products, including non-slip materials*
	—		
Industrial Scotch-brite Products	—		
		—	
Disposable Products		—	

3 You will now hear Mr Johnson describing his present position. As you listen, take notes and then write a short description of his job and responsibilities. After you have done this, refer back to the organisation chart and identify the person in the US with whom Mr Johnson is most likely to be in regular contact.

SPEAKING

1 Work in pairs (Student A and Student B). Student A should look at the information below and Student B at the information on page 146.

Student A
Read the following profile and be ready to play the role of Susan Robertson. Prepare a list of questions that you will need to ask Giancarlo Peretto (played by Student B) in order to complete his profile. Then take it in turns to interview each other.

Examples: *How long have you been with your present company?*
What are you responsible for?

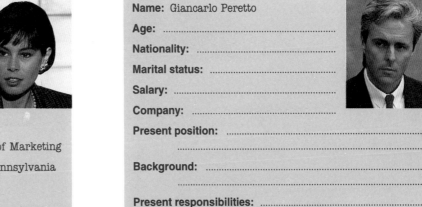

Name: Susan Robertson

Age: 29

Nationality: American

Marital status: Single

Salary: $38,000 per annum

Company: US Brands Incorporated

Present position: • Brand Manager
• Works under the Director of Marketing

Background: • MBA from the University of Pennsylvania
• Joined the company in 1991

Present responsibilities:
• In charge of determining national marketing strategy for a brand of paper towels
• Heads a business team of 10 people which studies consumers' opinions of company products

Name: Giancarlo Peretto

Age: ....

Nationality: ....

Marital status: ....

Salary: ....

Company: ....

Present position: ....

Background: ....
....

Present responsibilities: ....
....
....
....
....

2 Work in pairs again. Student A should look at the information below, and Student B at the information on page 146.

Student A
Read the following company profile and study the kind of information it contains.
Be prepared to answer questions about it.

The MoDo Group is an international company. Its headquarters are in Stockholm. The President and Chief Executive Officer is Bernt Lof. Its main areas of business are fine paper, newsprint and magazine paper and other wood products. Most of MoDo's production is carried out in Sweden, but the company is present in many European countries and in the United States. More than 80% of the Group's total sales of 18.4 million Swedish kronor in 1990 came from countries outside Sweden, primarily the European Community. The company has about 12,961 employees.

Now ask your partner questions to obtain similar information about the company that he or she has been working on, and complete the notes below.

Name of company ....

Headquarters ....

Chairman ....

Business activities ....

Main markets ....

Sales in 1991 ....

No. of employees ....

WRITING   Write a short profile about ICI, using the information provided below. Use the MoDo and Virgin Group profiles as models.

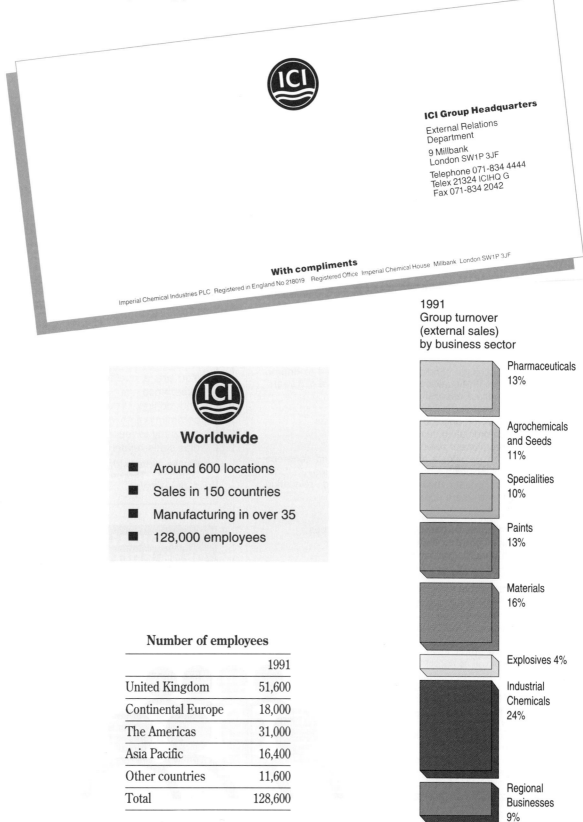

ICI Group Headquarters

External Relations
Department

9 Millbank
London SW1P 3JF

Telephone 071-834 4444
Telex 21324 ICIHQ G
Fax 071-834 2042

With compliments   Imperial Chemical House Millbank London SW1P 3JF

Imperial Chemical Industries PLC Registered in England No 218019   Registered Office Imperial Chemical House Millbank London SW1P 3JF

Worldwide

■ Around 600 locations

■ Sales in 150 countries

■ Manufacturing in over 35

■ 128,000 employees

Number of employees

	1991
United Kingdom	51,600
Continental Europe	18,000
The Americas	31,000
Asia Pacific	16,400
Other countries	11,600
Total	128,600

1991
Group turnover
(external sales)
by business sector

Pharmaceuticals 13%

Agrochemicals and Seeds 11%

Specialities 10%

Paints 13%

Materials 16%

Explosives 4%

Industrial Chemicals 24%

Regional Businesses 9%

Recruitment

KEY VOCABULARY

When a company needs to **recruit** or employ new people, it may decide to advertise the job or **position** in the **appointments page** of a newspaper. People who are interested can then **apply** for the job by sending in a **letter of application** and **curriculum vitae** containing details of their education and experience. The company will then draw up a **shortlist** of **candidates**, who are invited to attend an **interview**.

LEAD-IN

1 Look at the five job advertisements below and the extracts from five letters of application on the following page. Match each letter with the corresponding advertisement.

1

We are a leading firm of Chartered Accountants and are presently seeking a

HUMAN RESOURCES MANAGER

The successful candidate will be educated to degree level with IPM qualifications and a minimum of 3 years' experience. Responsibilities will include:
- developing policies and procedures
- advising on aspects of employment law
- co-ordinating training programmes
- recruitment selection

In return we offer a competitive salary and generous benefits including a non-contributory pension, 25 days' holiday, private health insurance, and relocation assistance where appropriate.

Apply with CV and covering letter to:
Sally Fraser, Director of Human Resources, Brooks Thornton & Co., Norfolk House, 153 Aldwych, London WC2B 4JY.

2

OPERATIONS OFFICER

International children's charity with headquarters in New York and offices throughout the world has an opening for an operations officer to fill a position in Mali. The successful candidate will be responsible for all aspects of the management of this office. He or she should possess an advanced university degree in business administration or a related qualification and should have at least five years' experience in office management at international level. Fluency in English and French is essential. Willingness to travel and live and work under difficult conditions. Benefits include a competitive international salary and overseas allowances.

Please write with your CV and stating current salary to: Box number RL 147, The Guardian, 164 Deansgate, Manchester M60 2RR

3

SENIOR PRODUCTION MANAGER

Electronic and Optical Equipment

You are a qualified engineer with several years' experience of computer assisted technology and design. Your proven managerial skills and commitment to quality will enable this expanding company to reach its full potential. Excellent salary plus sales-related bonus and company car.

Please write with full CV to: John Hart, Redwood Marshall, Thorpe Industrial Estate, Crabtree Rd, Feltham TW14.

4

MEDICAL DESK EDITOR

Science graduate required to work on medical journal. Editorial experience desirable but not essential as full training given.

Excellent prospects. Subsidised staff canteen.

Apply in writing to Jonathan Shepherd, Editorial Director, Williams & Faulkner Ltd., 18 Marryat Rd, London SW19.

5

CUSTOMER SERVICES ASSISTANT

Are you highly efficient with good communication and inter-personal skills? We are a leading manufacturer of video and audio equipment, and are looking for someone special with good administrative and secretarial abilities to join our very busy Customer Services Department. Salary dependent on age and experience.

Apply to: Brenda Howarth, Spectro (UK) Ltd., 12 Rothesay Terrace, Edinburgh EH3 7SE.

a

The management experience that I acquired during my six years with the Council for Economic Affairs has equipped me to deal with the various demands of an international organisation. During my time with the Council I was in charge of the finance, accounts and administration of our Asian operations.

b

During my time at Manchester, I worked on a number of university magazines and this has made me keen to pursue a career in publishing.

c

I have good office and word-processing skills which I would like to put to use in a more interesting and challenging role. I enjoy working in a team and dealing with the public as well.

d

My current position involves me in all aspects of personnel, with particular emphasis on interviewing, induction and organizing training courses.

e

As you will see from the attached cv, I am presently responsible for managing a sophisticated manufacturing site with a staff of thirty.

2 Read through the advertisements again and make a list of all the words and expressions used to describe a) the job requirements, and b) the benefits offered by the job.

	Requirements	Benefits
e.g.	*educated to degree level*	*competitive salary*

3 Working in groups, discuss the following statements. Which ones do you agree or disagree with? Present your views to the class.

‘Married men with children and financial responsibilities make the best candidates.’

‘Women are less reliable than men and can cause problems for any department.’

‘Candidates who have frequently changed jobs are always valuable because of their experience.’

‘Tarot card readings and astrologers’ reports play a useful role in the recruitment process.’

‘A good salary is the best way to get people interested in their jobs.’

READING

According to the text below, are the following statements true or false?

	T	F
1		
2		
3		
4		
5		

1 Good-looking people are often more successful than others.

2 British Airways does not allow its pilots to work if they are 20 per cent overweight.

3 Attractive women have problems reaching managerial positions.

4 Morphopsychology is sometimes used as the only criterion when selecting candidates.

5 Employers' attitudes to 'unfair' recruitment practices have not changed.

LOOKS: *Appearance Counts With Many Managers*

By Sherry Buchanan
International Herald Tribune

London – There is something downright undemocratic about judging managers' abilities on the color of their eyes, the size of their lips, the shape of their noses or the amount of their body fat. Yet looks matter a lot more in hiring and promotions than employers will admit to others, or even to themselves.

Airlines and police forces have long had height and/or weight requirements for their staff, arguing that being physically fit and strong – not too fat or too small – is in the interest of the public's safety. In some cases, unhappy employees are challenging the arbitrary rules, which have been used by the airlines to recruit only good-looking women; in other cases, employers are trying to be fairer to avoid lawsuits.

Scotland Yard requires its male employees to be at least 5 feet 8 inches (1.73 meters) tall and female employees to be at least 5 feet 4 inches. The Yard decided to accept shorter women a few years ago to conform with Britain's equal-opportunity rules.

Air France still requires its female cabin crew to be between 1.58 meters and 1.78 meters, and men to be between 1.70 meters and 1.92 meters. They must also have a "harmonious silhouette." And British Airways grounds any member of its cabin crew – pilots

excluded – if they are 20 per cent over the average weight for their height.

Being short or overweight may affect people's careers in other industries in more subtle ways.

"I used to do all my business on the phone when I was a manager in my twenties, because there I could command great authority," said Ilona Morgan of the Equal Opportunities Commission in Manchester, who is 5 feet tall.

Being too small and or overweight is only one way that looks can have an impact on someone's career. Academic research at Edinburgh University, New York University and Utah State University shows that the better-looking a person is, the more positive qualities they are thought to have and the more positive impact that has in a career.

There is some evidence, however, that women who are too attractive – unless they are television commentators or have other high-visibility jobs – do not rank well as managers.

"There is enough research now to conclude that attractive women who aspire to managerial positions do not fare as well as women who may be less attractive," said Gerald Adams, a professor at Utah State University and an authority on the subject.

Some French employers and recruiters decide whether a manager is right for the job based upon looks. In some cases, morphopsychologists – a term coined by a French neuropsychiatrist in 1935 – attempt to determine personality traits according to a job applicant's face, eyes, mouth, nose, ears and hands.

"Unfortunately, morphopsychology has become a criterion for recruitment in France," said Bruno Vincenti with the Centre des Jeunes Dirigeants in Paris, the French employers' organization. "When it is used as the sole criterion, it is a catastrophe."

"Some people hire you because of the color of your tie; why not the shape of your ears?" said Frederique Rollet, a psychotherapist in Paris who is the author of several books on morphopsychology.

DISCUSSION

1 Do you think a certain type of appearance is necessary for some jobs? Explain why.

2 In your opinion, is morphopsychology a useful recruitment technique?

3 How are employment practices monitored in your country? Give examples.

VOCABULARY

1 Match the words from the text with their corresponding definitions.

1	to matter (*line 6*)	**a**	a person that you work for
2	to hire (*line 6*)	**b**	to need
3	promotion (*line 7*)	**c**	characteristics
4	employer (*line 7*)	**d**	the long-term plan for your professional life
5	to require (*line 10*)	**e**	to put in order of importance
6	career (*line 37*)	**f**	to be important
7	authority (*line 42*)	**g**	to give employment to someone
8	qualities (*line 52*)	**h**	a person who applies for a job
9	to rank (*line 59*)	**i**	the power to give orders
10	applicant (*line 73*)	**j**	a movement to a more important job, with more responsibility and money

2 Complete the following passage about the role of headhunters in business, using words from the previous exercise. Change the form of the words where necessary.

Headhunters, or executive search firms, specialise in finding the right person for the right job. When a company wishes to ¹.............................. a person for an important position, it may use the services of such a firm, specifying the skills and ².............................. which it ³.............................. of the future employee.

The headhunter contacts executives with the right ⁴.............................. profile, and provides the company with a shortlist of suitable candidates. In this way, the ⁵.............................. does not have to go through the preliminary stages of interviewing and selecting ⁶.............................. itself.

LANGUAGE FOCUS

PRESENT SIMPLE AND PRESENT CONTINUOUS

Look at the following sentences.

1 Scotland Yard requires its male employees to be at least 1.73 m tall.
2 We're recruiting more and more graduates.
3 Who is she talking to?
4 I'm meeting the Production Manager this afternoon.
5 The train leaves at 6.00 tomorrow evening.
6 James is working at home until the new office is ready.
7 I get up at 7.00 most mornings.

Which sentence refers to:

a a temporary situation
b an action that is happening now
c a permanent state or situation
d a future arrangement
e a regular or habitual action
f a changing and developing situation
g a future event based on a timetable?

Which tense is used in each case?

➤➤ For more information on the present simple and present continuous, turn to page 153.

Practice This is part of a report that a Personnel Manager wrote after interviewing a candidate for the position of Director of Software Engineering. Put the verbs in brackets into the present simple or present continuous tense.

Interview assessment

Articulate and well presented, Paul Sutherland is an excellent candidate for the post of Director of Software Engineering.

He [1] .... (want) to leave his present employer, a small computer company, because he [2] .... (feel) that he [3] .... (not use) his knowledge of software engineering to the full. He [4] .... (look for) a more challenging position where his field of specialisation can be exploited in a more stimulating environment. He [5] .... (realise) that our company [6] .... (grow) rapidly, and that he would be expected to contribute to that growth. He is familiar with our existing range of software and regularly [7] .... (read) our publications.

Although at present he [8] .... (live) in the south he [9] .... (say) that he is willing to go wherever we [10] .... (decide) to send him. He occasionally [11] .... (travel) to various European countries for trade fairs and exhibitions and [12] .... (enjoy) meeting people of different nationalities. At the moment he [13] .... (attend) a training course at the Goethe Institute in order to perfect his German.

Mr Sutherland [14] .... (go away) tomorrow for two weeks. I [15] .... (suggest) that we contact him on his return to offer him a second interview.

SKILLS FOCUS

READING Look at the job advertisement and answer the questions.

1 Who placed the job advertisement in the newspaper?
2 What job is being offered?
3 In what sector of business?
4 What is required for the job?
5 Where will the successful candidate work?
6 Where are the company's headquarters?

"PREFER A CAMPING TRIP TO A COCKTAIL PARTY?"

PATAGONIA has a new position open:
PUBLIC AFFAIRS ASSOCIATE

Job is based in Munich. Candidates must have substantial PR/Press experience and strong writing skills. They must have serious proficiency in technical sports (skiing, kayaking, climbing ...) and outdoor experience. German mother tongue. Environmental background a plus. No glamor ... it's a gritty job! Patagonia is a Californian company which designs and distributes functional outdoor clothing. Send CV with picture to:

Nathalie Baudoin
PATAGONIA GMBH
Reitmorstrasse 50
8000 Munich 22 – Germany

The interviews will be in Munich during the last week of February.

patagonia®

PREPARATION FOR WRITING

1 The curriculum vitae

Fiona Scott is one of the applicants for the job at Patagonia. Study her CV carefully to see how the information is presented and decide where each of the following headings should be placed.

REFERENCES	INTERESTS	PERSONAL DETAILS
PROFESSIONAL EXPERIENCE	EDUCATION	ADDITIONAL SKILLS

CURRICULUM VITAE

1 ....

Name:	Fiona Scott
Date of Birth:	7 August 1969
Nationality:	British
Address:	52 Hanover Street
	Edinburgh EH2 5LM
	Scotland
Telephone:	031 449 0237

2 ....

1991–1992: London Chamber of Commerce and Industry
Diploma in Public Relations

1988–1991: University of London
BA (Honours) In Journalism and Media Studies (Class II)

1981–1988: Fettes College, Edinburgh
A-levels in German (A), English (B), History (B) and Geography (C)

3 ....

1992 to present: Scottish Wildlife Trust
Department of Public Relations

Responsible for writing articles on all aspects of the Trust's activities and ensuring their distribution to the press. Editor of the Trust's monthly journal. In charge of relations with European environmental agencies.

Summers of
1990 and 1991: Three-month training period with the Glasgow Herald. Assistant to the sports editor.

Summer of 1989: Sales assistant in the record department of Harris Stores Ltd., Edinburgh.

4 ....

Sports: Cross-country skiing, rock-climbing and swimming.
Secretary of the local branch of 'Action', an association organising summer camps for disabled children.

5 ....

Camp counselling certificate
Grade 3 ski instructor
Driver's licence (car and motorcycle)
IBM PC user
Fluent German and good working knowledge of French

6 ....

Geoffrey Williams,   Bill Denholm,
Professor of Journalism,   Sports Editor,
University of London   Glasgow Herald

Look back at sections 2 and 3. What do you notice about the order of dates?

2 The letter of application

The letter of application (also called the covering letter) can be as important as the CV in that it often provides the first direct contact between a candidate and an employer. If this letter is not well written and presented, it will make a poor impression. The letter of application normally contains three or more paragraphs in which you should:

- confirm that you wish to apply and say where you learned about the job
- say why you are interested in the position and relate your interests to those of the company
- show what you can contribute to the job by highlighting your most relevant skills and experience
- indicate your willingness to attend an interview (and possibly state when you would be free to attend)

Complete Fiona Scott's letter of application using the following verbs:

contact	discuss	employed	welcome	involved
apply	enjoy	notice	advertised	matches

Fiona Scott
52 Hanover Street
Edinburgh EH2 5LM
Scotland
UK
8th January

Nathalie Baudoin
Patagonia GMBH
Reitmorstrasse 50
8000 Munich 22
Germany

Dear Ms Baudoin,

I am writing to [1]............................... for the position of Public Affairs Associate which was [2]............................... last week in the International Herald Tribune.

Although I am presently [3]............................... by a non-profit making organisation, it has always been my intention to work in a commercial environment. I would particularly [4]............................... the chance to work for your company and as you will [5]............................... on my enclosed curriculum vitae, the job you are offering [6]............................... both my personal and professional interests.

My work experience has familiarised me with many of the challenges [7]............................... in public relations today. I am sure that this, together with my understanding of the needs and expectations of sport and nature enthusiasts, would be extremely relevant to the position. Moreover, as my mother is German, I am fluent in this language and would definitely [8]............................... working in a German-speaking environment.

I would be pleased to [9]............................... my curriculum vitae with you in more detail at an interview. In the meantime, please do not hesitate to [10]............................... me if you require further information. I look forward to hearing from you.

Yours sincerely,

Fiona Scott

Fiona Scott

3 Work in pairs. Refer back to the job advertisement, CV and letter of application. What do you think are Fiona Scott's chances of getting the job? What are her strengths and weaknesses?

WRITING The Renault car company is advertising for graduates to join its management programme. Read the advertisement carefully, then prepare the CV and letter of application that you would send to Sian Vernon. You may invent as many details as you wish, but note that the person who you present in your CV will not graduate until the end of this year.

THE SUNDAY TIMES   Sunday 15 March

GRADUATING ?

£13,500 + Car

Open the door to your career with Renault . . . and your first company car

The Graduate intake at Renault is always special. The challenge we have in store could mean rapid progression on a fast track to a position of real responsibility in our Sales, Marketing, Technical, Finance or Computing Departments after a full and realistic induction to the RENAULT philosophy of TOTAL QUALITY.

We have a proven track record of expertise in opening career doors for our Graduate Managers to reach the top. You will be expected to emulate their success.

Our key preferences are:

• A business related honours degree
• Numeracy
• Panache and business flair
• A good standard of French
• A robust and energetic character
• Prepared to travel
• Aged under 25

Successful applicants will have a job offer before the end of May.

Meanwhile write to – Sian Vernon, Personnel Officer, at the address shown. Tell me on one side of A4 paper why I should choose you. Please attach your CV, to arrive no later than Friday, 3rd April.

Please give a contact telephone number where you can be reached on Thursday, 9th April. Those selected for interview will be contacted on this date.

Renault UK Limited Western Avenue Acton London W3 0RZ
Tel: 081-992 3481 Fax: 081-993 2734

RENAULT UK LTD

21

LISTENING

You will hear David Smyth, the Personnel Manager of a major European insurance company, answering questions about the way he interviews and selects candidates.

1 In the first extract he talks about the four points listed below. Listen and put them in the order in which he talks about them.

a the mistakes a candidate can make in an interview
b the qualities a candidate must have
c his advice to interviewees
d the kind of things a candidate is expected to know

Listen again and take notes on each of these points.

2 In the second extract, David Smyth talks about the stages of an interview. Listen to what he says and complete the following flow chart:

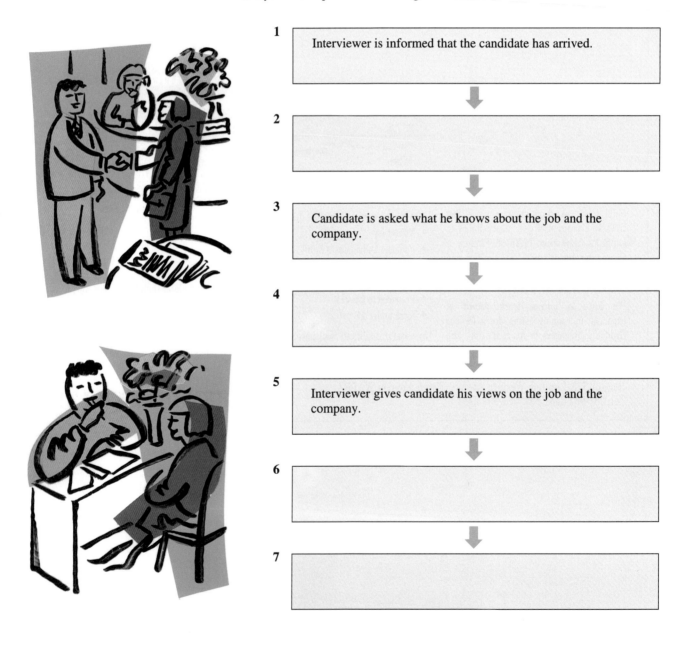

1 Interviewer is informed that the candidate has arrived.

2

3 Candidate is asked what he knows about the job and the company.

4

5 Interviewer gives candidate his views on the job and the company.

6

7

SPEAKING   Work in pairs (Student A and Student B). Student A should look at the information below, and Student B at the information on page 152.

Student A

You are Sian Vernon, Personnel Officer for Renault UK Ltd. You are going to interview a candidate (Student B) for a place on the graduate management programme, as described in the advertisement on page 21. First read the CV and letter of application which Student B will give you, and think about the questions which you would like to ask. Then conduct the interview using the flow chart on page 22 to help you.

When you have finished the interview, complete the following evaluation sheet for Student B. Would you employ him or her? Why?/Why not? Discuss your reasons with Student B.

EVALUATION SHEET

Position: ....

Name of candidate: ....

	Score
	− +
	1 2 3 4 5

BACKGROUND
Education:
Languages:
Experience:

BEHAVIOUR AND COMMUNICATIVE ABILITY
Physical Presentation:
Communication skills:
Ability to listen:
Humour:
Culture:
Maturity:
Manners:

PERSONAL QUALITIES
Dynamism:
Ambition:
Organisational Skills:
Leadership:
Team Spirit:
Involvement:

CONCLUSION

Suitability of the candidate: ....

....

....

Action to be taken: ....

....

Management Styles

KEY VOCABULARY

The amount of responsibility of any individual in a company depends on the position that he or she occupies in its hierarchy. Managers, for example, are responsible for leading the people directly under them, who are called **subordinates**. To do this successfully, they must use their **authority**, which is the right to take the decisions and give the orders that will allow their subordinates to reach certain objectives. Managers often **delegate** authority. This means that employees at lower levels of the company hierarchy can participate in decision-making.

LEAD-IN

1 The characteristics of management often vary according to national culture, which can determine how managers are trained, how they lead people and how they approach their jobs.

Below and on the following page you will find five brief portraits of managers in five different countries. Using your knowledge of the United States, the United Kingdom, France, Germany and Sweden, decide which country each of these portraits corresponds to.

1

Managers from this country:

- consider professional and technical skills to be very important.

- have a strong sense of authority.

- respect the different positions in the hierarchy of their companies.

- clearly define how jobs should be done.

- are very loyal to their companies and expect their subordinates to obey them.

- are often older than in other countries.

2

Managers from this country:

- receive a general education.

- delegate authority.

- take a practical approach to management.

- have relatively formal relationships at work.

- encourage their employees to work individually.

- believe it is important to continue education and training at work.

3

Managers from this country:

- consider social qualities to be as important as education.

- encourage their employees to take an interest in their work.

- pay close attention to the quality of working life.

- do not use as much authority as in other countries.

- appreciate low-level decision-making.

- are often women.

4

Managers from this country:

- generally attend business schools.

- communicate easily and informally at work.

- admire the qualities of a leader.

- expect everyone to work hard. Individual performance is measured and initiative is rewarded.

- have competitive and sometimes aggressive attitudes towards work.

- often accept innovation and change.

5

Managers from this country:

- go through an elitist educational system.

- have a strong sense of hierarchy and power.

- often have impersonal relationships at work.

- analyse problems in great detail before taking decisions.

- consider speaking skills to be particularly important.

- move easily between state and private sectors.

2 In groups, discuss the advantages and disadvantages of each approach to management, and say which one you would find the most attractive. Do any of these profiles correspond to management practices in your country?

Be nice and smile if you want to hire a Hungarian manager

European executive profiles
● **Steve Lodge** in London

Eastern Europe is no more a block than Western Europe when it comes to the way managers think, according to research by an Anglo-Dutch joint venture. Questionnaires completed by 8,000 managers from 18 European countries – including 400 each from Poland, Hungary, Bulgaria and East Germany – show that 40 years of Communism has distorted but not overridden national cultures.

For instance, Bulgarians are just as unlikely to help the boss paint his house at the weekend as their UK, Dutch or West German counterparts. But nearly a third of Hungarians, a similar proportion to that in Spain or Italy, would do so. 'This should explode the myth of an Eastern bloc – all countries are different,' says David Wheatley of British-based Employment Conditions abroad, which has developed the original research of Fons Trompenaars of the Centre for International Business Studies in the Netherlands.

Mr Wheatley believes the research, which he plans to publish soon, should help West European companies employing and doing business with East Europeans. Deep-seated differences in attitude could be crucial to the way companies judge potential recruits, business partners and suppliers, as well as the ability to win business. Unless you recognise and take into account the differences, business relationships will falter or even fail, he says.

A Pole will call you utterly crazy during a meeting without meaning to be personal. Criticism of an idea does not extend to the person any more than it does among the Irish, the research finds. But East Germans and Hungarians are evenly matched between those who can take it and those who fear losing face. But all will take criticism of their plans better than Greeks, Portuguese, Spaniards and Italians, the research finds.

A Hungarian manager is as likely to join your company because he likes and respects you, as much as the career opportunity itself. So friendly interviewing might pay off in recruitment. Colder, more formal work relationships – as in West Germany or Austria – might suit East Germans better.

Nine out of ten Hungarians will expect to be judged on the basis of who they are, rather than what they do. Austrians are similar. And in contrast to other East Europeans and his Greek neighbours, the typical Bulgarian expects to be judged more on how he works.

Surprisingly, the research finds East European managers are less collective thinkers than the West Germans, Belgians or French. Individual bonuses might motivate managers from Hungary, Bulgaria, Poland and East Germany better than many Westerners.

More than half East German managers questioned thought the overwhelming goal of a company should be profit. This is the greatest proportion of any country – West or East – and compares with only a quarter of West Germans and one in eight Hungarians. And three-quarters of East German managers also believe in getting the job done, no matter how upsetting this may be for employees.

Both these attitudes should bode well for the restructuring of East German industry into a united German economy with its associated redundancies. But West Germans might find East Germans' distrust of 'the system' hard to handle. East Germans would lie to protect their friends rather than follow the rules, and might in turn question the West Germans' own values.

But having ditched the emotional baggage of Communism, other East European managers might still not be left with anything like Anglo-Saxon business values. Hungarian and Polish managers will be much more loathe to sack people to rationalise their industry than East Germans. Three out of five Hungarian managers would favour adjusting their enterprises' objectives, including profits, to spare existing workers. Mr Wheatley says the more Catholic countries might retain a view of business modelled more around personal relationships than Western business values.

National barriers may well be replaced with cultural ones, the research warns. If that is the case companies should prepare themselves for business values as different as those between Latin and Anglo-Saxon countries in the West.

The European

READING

Read the text on the opposite page and complete the following table.

✓ = Managers in this country are more likely to …
✗ = Managers in this country are less likely to …

(— = Answer not given in text)

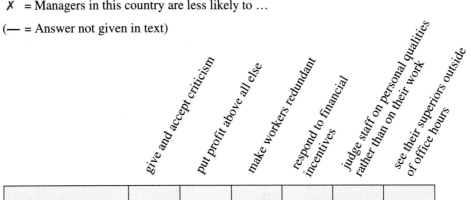

	give and accept criticism	put profit above all else	make workers redundant	respond to financial incentives	judge staff on personal qualities rather than on their work	see their superiors outside of office hours
Hungary	—					
Bulgaria	—	—	—			
Poland		—				—
East Germany	—					—
West Germany	—		—	—	—	
Spain		—	—	—	—	
Italy		—	—	—		
Greece		—	—	—		—

VOCABULARY

1 Match the words from the text with their corresponding definitions.

1 profile (*subtitle*)   **a** a sum of money given in addition to a salary

2 attitude (*line 29*)   **b** an assembly of people, especially for discussion

3 relationship (*line 34*)   **c** to tell an employee that he/she must leave his/her job

4 meeting (*line 37*)   **d** to make something more efficient

5 suit (*line 53*)   **e** to be right or convenient for

6 bonus (*line 64*)   **f** reductions in the number of employees

7 motivate (*line 64*)   **g** the connection between two or more people

8 redundancies (*line 80*)   **h** to stimulate someone to take an interest in something

9 rule (*line 84*)   **i** a statement which tells you what you should or must do

10 sack (*line 91*)   **j** a description of a person's characteristics

11 rationalise (*line 92*)   **k** a way of thinking or behaving

2 Find words in the text to describe a person who:

1 lives next to you = *a neighbour* (*line 58*)

2 does the same job as someone else in a different place or organisation

3 is from the West, especially Europe or North America

4 is employed by a company, but who has no management responsibility

5 is in charge of a business or department

6 has recently joined a company

7 sells goods or equipment to a company

8 shares the responsibility of owning and running a business

3 Complete the following passage using words from the left-hand column of exercise 1 and words that you found in exercise 2. Change the form of the words where necessary.

Motivating a multinational team

Several organisations have been carrying out research to determine the best way to
[1]........................... a multinational team of employees. The results of this work show
that the principal problems are caused by cultural differences. For example, one
study, in which members of ten nationalities attended regular [2]...........................
together, revealed that the French could not understand the practical British
[3]........................... to conducting business, which they thought indicated a lack of
preparation. On the other hand, the Americans found it difficult to accept shaking
hands with the French every morning, which they saw as a sign of a more formal
[4]........................... .

Language can also cause misunderstandings: take the case of an American
[5]........................... who wrote 'quite good' on a report prepared by his British
subordinate. This was interpreted as meaning 'not very good' when in fact the
American had meant 'better than good'.

To overcome these problems, the successful multinational team should be composed
of managers who have the right [6]........................... in terms of attitude and
experience and who [7]........................... the positions that they are appointed to. It
should also be a team that understands the basic [8]........................... that 'difference'
should be accepted.

LANGUAGE FOCUS

ADJECTIVES OF NATIONALITY

Study the following examples from the text:

Country: ... *Managers from 18 European countries – including 400 each from* **Poland** ... (line 6)

Inhabitant: *A* **Pole** *will call you utterly crazy during a meeting without meaning to be personal.* (line 36)

Nationality: ... **Polish** *managers will be much more loathe to sack people* ... (line 90)

Practice

Match the words from each list below to make as many sentences as you can. You will have to transform the names of the countries into adjectives of nationality.

Example: *IBM is an* **American** *computer company.*

1	Philips	Denmark	furniture retailer
2	Mateus Rosé	Norway	newspaper
3	BBC 1	France	computer company
4	Ferrari	Holland	beer
5	IBM	Spain	electronics company
6	AGFA	Finland	watch
7	Cambio 16	USA	industrial company
8	Carlsberg	UK	mineral water
9	IKEA	Switzerland	seaport
10	Evian	Turkey	airline
11	Olympic	Portugal	car manufacturer
12	Rolex	Russia	photographic company
13	Pravda	Germany	wine
14	Aker AS	Greece	chemical company
15	Istanbul	Italy	weekly magazine
16	Neste	Sweden	television channel

EXPRESSING FRACTIONS AND PROPORTIONS

Study the following examples and note how fractions are expressed in English:

A/one **quarter** *of our employees speak a foreign language.* (= 25%)
A/one **third** *of our employees are women.* (= 33.3%)
A/one **half** *of our employees go on holiday in August.* (= 50%)

Note that it is not necessary to use *a* or *one* before *half*. The third example above could also read:

Half *of our employees go on holiday in August.*

Other commonly used fractions in English are:

1/10 = *a/one tenth*
1/5 = *a/one fifth*
2/3 = *two thirds*
3/4 = *three quarters*

We can also use the following constructions to express proportion:

Nine **out of** *ten graduates have already found employment.* (= 90%)
By the year 2000, one **in** *five cars in this country will be Korean.* (=20%)

Practice

1 Find expressions in the text which mean the same as the following percentages.

Example: 30% - *nearly a third* (line 15)

1	75%	**4**	60%
2	50%+	**5**	90%
3	12.5%	**6**	25%

2 Study the following pie charts which show the results of a recent survey of America's top chief executives. Then complete the passage with an appropriate fraction or proportion. Do not use percentages.

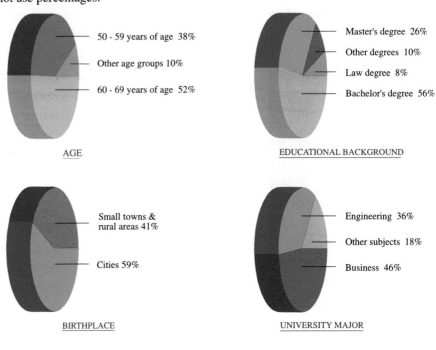

50 - 59 years of age 38%

Other age groups 10%

60 - 69 years of age 52%

AGE

Master's degree 26%

Other degrees 10%

Law degree 8%

Bachelor's degree 56%

EDUCATIONAL BACKGROUND

Small towns & rural areas 41%

Cities 59%

BIRTHPLACE

Engineering 36%

Other subjects 18%

Business 46%

UNIVERSITY MAJOR

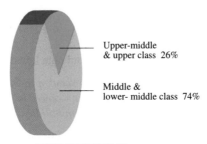

Upper-middle & upper class 26%

Middle & lower- middle class 74%

SOCIAL BACKGROUND

Source : Business Horizons

One of the most striking findings of the survey is that only [1]................................. of America's top chief executives is below the age of 50. The survey also reveals that the executives have very different educational backgrounds: just over [2]................................. hold a Bachelor's degree, approximately [3]................................. obtained a Master's degree, and the others hold either law degrees, doctorates or other types of degree. As undergraduates, just under [4]................................. of the executives chose to study business, more than [5]................................. studied engineering and the rest some other subject. It is interesting to note that about [6]................................. of these top executives come from middle to lower-middle class backgrounds and that nearly [7]................................. were born in cities.

SKILLS FOCUS

LISTENING

You will hear Tom Scheck, one of the directors of Profile, an international business consultancy, talking about his company and some of the problems involved in international negotiations.

1 Listen carefully to the first extract and answer the questions below.

1 Why was Profile set up?
2 What information does Profile provide?

2 In the second extract, you will hear Mr Scheck giving advice on how to succeed in an international business context. First study the structures in bold in each of the sentences below. Then listen to the cassette to complete the sentences.

1 **It is important to** remember that every country has its own .... which defines the context.

2 **You should always** .... this context when doing business ....

3 **Don't forget that** .... in different environments.

4 **It is also important to** remember when you .... that he is sending out signals which could help you greatly in your .... with him.

5 **You should always** avoid thinking that your local partner is .... than you are.

6 **It is essential to** be ....

7 **You have to** .... for each market.

3 To illustrate how values can change from country to country, Mr Scheck uses the example of selling a car. Listen to the third extract and complete the table below.

In France cars are presented in terms of:	In Holland cars are presented in terms of:
a...	a...
b...	b...

4 In the final extract Mr Scheck talks about doing business in Eastern Europe. Listen and decide if the following statements are true or false.

	T	F
1 There are no differences between Eastern European and Western European styles of doing business.		
2 Forty years of communism has had an effect on the systems of management in Eastern Europe.		
3 The market research carried out by Profile shows that the systems of distribution in Eastern Europe do not work.		
4 Some Eastern European countries are more developed than others.		
5 If you are not well informed about local cultures, you will never convince your partner of your professionalism.		

SPEAKING

Cultural differences

Many managers agree that an understanding of cultural differences is essential when doing business abroad. The following case studies illustrate what happens if business people do not take into account the culture of the countries they are dealing with.

1 In groups, read each of the four case studies. Choose one and discuss what you think caused the problem or misunderstanding.

1

Mr Byrd was an ex-US State Department employee hired by a well-known multinational corporation to be its 'man in Riyadh,' Saudi Arabia. This retired American diplomat went to the home of a Saudi, Mr Fouad, to try to interest him in participating in a local joint venture with his company. A middleman who knew them both had introduced them. As this was a first meeting, the men's conversation began with small talk that made Mr Byrd a little impatient.

Questions such as 'how are you doing? how was your flight? how is your family? and how is your father?' were common. Mr Byrd, familiar with all these obligatory formalities of greeting, answered 'fine.' 'Oh, my father, yes, well, he is fine, but he is getting a little deaf. I saw him a few months ago during Christmas when we took him out of the nursing home for a few days.' From that point everything froze up. Mr Byrd's mission was completely derailed. Mr Fouad remained gracious enough but was obviously uninterested in doing any business with Mr Byrd.

2

This incident was reported by a British management consultant based in Paris:

'I had taken the American CEO of a New York-based consulting company to a first meeting with the three partners of a French consulting firm in Paris. The negotiations did not go well. He hadn't been in the boardroom for more than 15 minutes before he asked them what their company's annual earnings were. Without waiting for an answer to that question, he suggested they give him an estimate of their firm's market value, as he was interested in making them an offer.

I could feel things freezing over.'

4

WHY IS NO ONE EATING?

A businesswoman recently asked why a high-level delegation of visiting Japanese clients had not approached the breakfast buffet table she had taken such great pains to prepare. 'I'd gotten out the good china and silverware and even brought in Japanese green tea for them, but no one touched a thing!'

3

Jim Turner was attending a conference in Lyons. This was not his first trip to France, and he was pleased some of the French colleagues he'd met previously remembered him. One evening they invited him along for dinner and began joking about the quality of the food. That surprised him. He thought the food was really rather good and said so, expecting the discussion to continue. But to his great discomfort, they then made some joke about 'food and Americans' and changed the subject. He felt somewhat excluded and didn't know what he'd done wrong.

2 Present your interpretation of the case to see if the rest of the class agrees with it. Could these situations cause conflict or misunderstanding in your country?

ROLE PLAY   **Giving and asking for advice**

Work in pairs. One person should look at the instructions below, and the other at the instructions on page 148. After working on your part for ten minutes, act out the dialogue.

> **Student A:**
> You are a cross-cultural consultant hired by a foreign executive going to do business for the first time in your country or a country you know well. Prepare some advice that you would give your client about business practices. Use the following topics to help you.
>
> **Use of language:** Is there a special way of addressing (or greeting) people? (Formal? Informal?)
>
> **Non-verbal communication:** What are the various roles played by handshaking, gestures, and silence.
>
> **Business negotiations:** How important is punctuality and respecting the agenda? What kind of negotiating styles are preferred? (Direct? Indirect?) When is the right moment to mention money?
>
> **Socialising:** What are the attitudes towards gift giving, eating and humour? What kind of conversation topics are avoided? (Religion? Politics? Salaries?)
>
>
>
> The following structures will help you to answer the questions that your client (Student B) will ask.
>
> *You should always/never …*
> *I would advise you to …*
> *Don't forget to …*
> *It is important/essential to …*
> *It would be a good idea to …*

WRITING   Look back at the text on page 26 and answer the following questions in two to three lines.

1   'Criticism of an idea does not extend to the person' (*para. 4*). How do you react to criticism of your ideas? Are you easily offended by criticism?

2   In your opinion, what should be the main objectives of a company?

3   What is a 'cultural barrier' (*para. 11*)? Have you ever been in a situation in which a difference in culture created a problem? Explain.

Advertising and Marketing

KEY VOCABULARY

Marketing is the term given to the different activities involved in distributing goods from the manufacturer to the final customer. The combination of the different elements of a company's marketing plan, such as product conception and development, promotion, pricing and packaging is known as the **marketing mix**.

Advertising is an important element of the marketing function. It is used to increase sales by making the product or service known to a wider audience, and by emphasising its superior qualities. A company can advertise in a variety of ways, depending on how much it wishes to spend, and the size and type of the **target audience**. The different media for advertising include television, radio, newspapers, magazines and direct mail, by which advertisers send letters, brochures and leaflets directly to potential customers.

Advertising is a highly developed business. In the UK, for example, approximately £5 billion is spent on advertising each year.

LEAD-IN

1 What other methods of advertising can you think of, apart from those listed above? In groups, make a list of the different media that are used to sell the following well-known products in your country.

2 Many advertisements contain a **slogan** or short phrase to attract the consumer's attention. Effective slogans are usually short, easy to remember and easy to repeat. Here are several authentic slogans from advertisements. What type of product do you think each one is advertising?

- ▢ Not everyone was meant to fly.
- ▢ The colour of life.
- ▢ Doesn't he deserve a dinner that looks as good as yours?
- ▢ By the time you remember you left it on, it's off.
- ▢ See and be seen with.
- ▢ Does she or doesn't she?
- ▢ This year you should wear something loud.
- ▢ Doesn't your family deserve less?
- ▢ Introducing seven easy ways to make a chicken fly.
- ▢ The best things in life are still made by hand.
- ▢ Never before has something so little done so much for so many.

3 **Endorsement** is a commonly used advertising technique, in which a person – often famous – speaks on behalf of a product.

Give an example of one personality in your country from each of the following fields who endorses a product:

Field	Name	Product
Sports		
Entertainment		
Business		

In each case, do you think the right person was chosen to endorse the product? Present your findings to the class.

READING

The text on the following page describes how Japanese companies are using American and European stars to endorse their products.

1 Scan the text quickly and match the following stars with the product they endorse or have endorsed.

1 Woody Allen

2 John McEnroe

3 Roger Moore

4 Paul Newman

5 Arnold Schwarzenegger

6 Sylvester Stallone

7 Sting

a

b

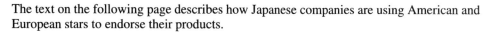
f

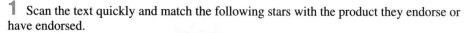
g

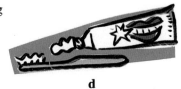
c
d

e

In Ads, US Stars Shine For Japanese Eyes Only

Top Dollar, and No Image Problems

By Margaret Shapiro
Washington Post Service

John McEnroe and his actress wife, Tatum O'Neal.

1 TOKYO — Dressed in a white tuxedo and red bow tie, Sylvester Stallone clearly has something important on his mind. But it's not Rocky or Rambo.

2 "Ito Ham," the American movie megastar says in the Japanese television commercial. "O-kay."

3 In the print version, Mr Stallone is even more eloquent about Ito's processed meat: "It is so delicious that it is a gift of love."

4 Mr Stallone is only one of many movie *su-tah*, as the Japanese call stars, showing up in advertisements these days. With companies paying top dollar and promising to run the ads only within the confines of this insular nation, Hollywood stars are eagerly appearing in commercials that they wouldn't be caught dead doing in the United States.

5 Paul Newman, for instance, hums in an elevator before letting viewers know that Fuji Bank's credit card is his "main card." Arnold Schwarzenegger, in excellent Japanese form, slurps up a mouthful of steaming Nissin instant noodles.

6 John McEnroe, the tennis player, and his actress wife, Tatum O'Neal, joke together in matching shirts while holding up a box of Assess toothpaste.

7 James Coburn and Roger Moore both "Speak Lark," the slogan used in ads here for Lark cigarettes. Even Woody Allen, the reclusive film director, once did a stint in Japanese advertising, appearing in a 1982 ad to promote the Seibu department store.

8 Movie stars rarely do commercials in the United States, lest it tarnish their image and their marketability. In the United States, getting into commercials is often a sign a career is on the way down.

9 But when it comes to Japan, said Irving Axelrad, a motion picture attorney, "I tell them to do it. They pay a lot of money and it's a couple of days."

10 Mr Axelrad and others protect their clients' American reputations by demanding that "Japan-only" clauses be written into advertising contracts. The clauses impose heavy penalties on Japanese companies if the ad somehow gets shown in the United States. Shinobu Ina, a casting manager at Dentsu Inc., Japan's largest advertising agency, said, "They want the money from appearing in the commercials but they don't want it known in the United States. They want to hide as much as possible that they are appearing in commercials in Japan."

11 Agents for several movie stars refused to comment, or never returned telephone calls. Japanese companies were equally leery of publicity. One company spokesman, after first demanding anonymity for himself and his firm, would only say, "Our star hates to be mentioned."

12 Nobody would discuss the fees paid to specific celebrities, although ad executives in Tokyo said well-known American or European actors make between $500,000 and $1 million, with the heftiest pay going to only a few major stars, like Mr Newman or the British rock star, Sting, who appears in ads on behalf of Kirin beer.

13 According to Mr Ina at Dentsu, American stars have been appearing in Japanese commercials since the 1950s. At that time they were the ultimate status symbol, since only a few companies could afford them. Instead, most relied on Japanese actors and actresses, who routinely appear in commercials.

14 "When we heard we needed $1 million, well, we thought that is really a lot of money," he said.

15 But the world has changed. The dollar has plummeted in the last four years, and so American movie stars, like US golf courses and office buildings, have become quite reasonably priced in yen terms.

16 In fact, Mr Ina notes, the money is no longer a problem. The problem is finding enough stars.

International Herald Tribune

2 Read the text in more detail and choose the best answer.

1 Which of the following statements is **not** one of the reasons why American stars are 'eagerly appearing' in Japanese commercials?

   a The stars are paid large sums of money.

   b The commercials are only run in Japan.

   c The stars are later asked to make films in Japan.

2 What do American stars endorse in Japanese commercials?

   a Both products and services.

   b Consumer products only.

   c Services only.

3 Which of the following statements does **not** explain why American stars rarely appear in commercials in the United States?

   a They are not paid enough.

   b They are afraid that appearing in a commercial will harm their image.

   c In the United States, appearing in a commercial is the sign of a declining career.

4 Which of the following statements is true?

   a All actors are paid the same fees for appearing in Japanese commercials.

   b British stars can earn as much as American stars for appearing in Japanese commercials.

   c Sports celebrities are paid more than movie actors for appearing in Japanese commercials.

5 Complete the following sentence with the best answer:
In the 1950s, . . .

   a . . . there were no commercials in Japan.

   b . . . a few American stars appeared in Japanese commercials.

   c . . . only Japanese actors appeared in Japanese commercials.

VOCABULARY

1 Find words in the text which correspond to the following definitions.

1 to publish an advertisement in the press or to show it on television (*para. 4*)

2 an advertisement on radio or television (*para. 4*)

3 people who watch television (*para. 5*)

4 a phrase used in advertising to attract attention to the product (*para. 7*)

5 to speak in favour of something; to try to sell something by advertising (*para. 7*)

6 the perception the public has of a person or organisation (*para. 8*)

7 a person legally appointed to act for another; a lawyer (*para. 9*)

8 a person who pays for professional services (*para. 10*)

9 special terms or conditions in a contract or agreement (*para. 10*)

10 a sum of money to be paid when a contract is broken (*para. 10*)

11 a person who speaks as the representative of other people (*para. 11*)

12 a payment for professional or special services (*para. 12*)

13 a sign of wealth and importance in society (*para. 13*)

14 to fall suddenly and quickly (*para. 15*)

2 RXV, a major electronics company, has decided to advertise its latest wide-screen television. It has gone to several advertising agencies to see which one can best plan and create a successful campaign. An executive of one of these agencies has made a list of preliminary tasks that must be done before the agency submits its proposal to the advertiser.

Choose seven of the answers found in the previous exercise to fill in the missing words on the executive's list. You will need to use the plural form of some of the words.

- Obtain complete marketing information about the [1].............................'s product: advantages, disadvantages, competitors, etc. Define marketing objectives and advertising strategy.

- Meet with media department to select appropriate means of advertising: newspaper and magazine advertisements or television [2]............................. Decide how often the company should [3]............................. the advertisements in the Press or on television.

- Ask creative director to develop an advertising message. Define what type of [4]............................. should be written and which illustrations should be chosen.

- Meet with casting manager from production company to select a celebrity to [5]............................. the product in the advertising campaign. Prepare contracts for television production team and include special [6]............................. where necessary.

- Calculate [7]............................. to be paid by RXV for services provided.

DISCUSSION

1 What are the advantages and disadvantages of using famous people in advertising?

2 Do you identify with pop stars and movie actors?

3 How can endorsing a product be bad for a celebrity's reputation?

LANGUAGE FOCUS

GERUND AND INFINITIVE

Look at the following sentences from the text.

*In the US, **getting** into commercials is often a sign a career is on the way down.* (para. 8)
*Agents for several movie stars refused **to comment**.* (para.11)

- What form of the verb is used in (a) the first sentence, and (b) the second sentence?
- In which sentence is the verb used as a noun?

➤➤ For more information on the gerund and infinitive, turn to page 154.

Practice

1 Scan the text quickly and find four examples of gerunds used after the prepositions *before, while, by* and *after*.

2 Complete the following passage using a gerund or infinitive. Choose from the verbs in the boxes.

build
set up
run
bring
make
transform

decide
reflect
appear
create

return
change
expand
launch
drink

Coca-Cola and its advertising

John S. Pemberton invented Coca-Cola in 1886. His partner suggested
[1].............................. an advertisement for the drink in the Atlanta Journal that very year. In 1888, Asa Candler bought the Coca-Cola business and decided
[2]............................. the product known through signs, calendars and clocks. The company began [3]............................. its global network when Robert Woodruff was elected president of the company in 1923. He succeeded in [4]............................. Coca-Cola into a truly international product by [5]............................. a foreign department, which exported Coca-Cola to the Olympic Games in Amsterdam in 1928. During World War II, he promised [6]............................. Coca-Cola to every soldier in every part of the world.

Coca-Cola's advertising has always attempted [7]............................. changing contemporary lifestyles. [8]............................. an international advertising campaign requires the talents of professionals in many areas, and extensive testing and research are always done before [9]............................. which advertisements will finally be used. Celebrity endorsements have featured heavily – Cary Grant, Ray Charles and Whitney Houston are just three of the big name stars who have agreed
[10]............................. in Coca-Cola commercials.

After [11]............................. Diet Coke in 1982, the company saw its sales grow quickly. The drink is now the third most popular in the world. In 1985, the company tried [12]............................. the secret formula of Coca-Cola, but realised that Americans were very attached to the original recipe. The company listened to its consumers and quickly responded by [13]............................. the original formula to the market as 'Coca-Cola Classic'. Today, people in more than 160 countries around the globe enjoy [14]............................. Coca-Cola. It is asked for more than 524 million times a day in more than 80 languages. The company intends [15]............................. its global presence even further in the twenty-first century, particularly in developing markets.

SKILLS FOCUS

SPEAKING 1

Describing target markets

Marketing and advertising specialists must carry out research to determine what customers want and to develop products which satisfy customer needs. A group of customers which shares a common interest, need or desire is called a **market**. Companies must determine which market would be most likely to buy a certain product and aim all their marketing activities at this **target**. Specialists use many different methods to divide markets into precise groups.

1 Working with a partner, choose one of the advertisements below and decide what the target market is. Use the following questions to help you:

1 Where does the target live? (town, suburbs, rural area, etc.)

2 What is the target's age?
sex?
marital status?
income?
occupation?
level of education?

3 What is the target's social class? (working, middle, upper class, etc.)

4 How would you describe the target's personality and lifestyle?

5 What benefits do you think the target looks for in the product? (comfort, safety, esteem, luxury, etc.)

ONE OF WALKERS MORE SOPHISTICATED RESEARCH LABS.

Whenever we try something new, we take it down the road to our original Walkers retail store on High Street. We figure if our own neighbors can't tell us whether our products are good or bad, who can? If it's all gone by the end of the day, we consider it a pretty good sign.

THE TASTE OF PURE HEAVEN FROM THE SCOTTISH HIGHLANDS.

WALKERS SHORTBREAD

After four years of school, the backpack's in better shape than the student.

You're exposed to a lot in school. Your backpack's exposed to even more. But look at it this way. After four years, at least your parents will be able to recognize the bag.

2 Present your findings to the class. Use the following structures.

We think the advertisement is | *designed* | *for ...*
| *meant* |
| *intended* |
In our opinion, the advertisement is aimed at ...
The advertisement targets ...
We believe that the advertisement is trying to reach ...

SPEAKING 2

Analysing advertisements

Working in groups of three or four, look through some recent magazines and newspapers and find two advertisements for different brands of the same product. Use the following checklist to compare the two advertisements you have chosen.

- What are the target markets for the two advertisements?

- What benefits do the advertisements emphasise?

- Compare the language used in the slogans. Does it attract attention quickly? Is it humorous?

- What technique is used in the text (or **copy**) of each advertisement: is it factual, does it contain a celebrity endorsement, is there no text at all? Is the price mentioned?

- Comment on the artistic content of the advertisements (photography, special graphics, etc.)

- Which advertisement do you think will sell the most products? Which is the most creative? Is there anything you would change in either of the ads?

Once your group has answered these questions, present your analysis of the advertisements to the rest of the class and see if they agree with your interpretation. You can also present your findings in a short written composition. Be sure to attach the ads to your paper.

LISTENING

The Harley-Davidson Motor Company, whose headquarters are in Milwaukee, Wisconsin (USA), has been producing its famous motorcycles since 1903. Many people buy Harley-Davidsons because, by adding different accessories, they can create truly personalised motorcycles.

There are other reasons why people choose to buy Harley-Davidson motorcycles. Before you listen, discuss what you think these reasons are.

You will now hear Mr Manfred Kozlowsky, Manager of Public Relations, Advertising and Promotion of Harley-Davidson Europe, discussing several different aspects of his company.

1 Listen to the first extract and decide which of the following descriptions corresponds to the typical Harley-Davidson buyer.

a Most Harley-Davidson buyers are about 45 and live in cities.
b There is not really one type of Harley-Davidson buyer, but the average age is about 35.
c There is not really one type of Harley-Davidson buyer, but the average income is high.

2 Listen to the second extract and write down the two words which Mr Kozlowsky uses to describe Harley-Davidson's image throughout the world.

How does he define the company's marketing strategy?

3 You will now hear the speaker give a list of countries (other than the United States) which are big markets for Harley-Davidson. Which of the following countries does he mention?

Austria	Germany	Ireland	Poland
Belgium	Greece	Italy	Spain
France	Holland	Japan	United Kingdom

4 Before listening to the final extract, study the chart below and describe the evolution of the company's exports from 1985 to 1990. Does 19.3 thousand seem like a small number of motorcycles to you?

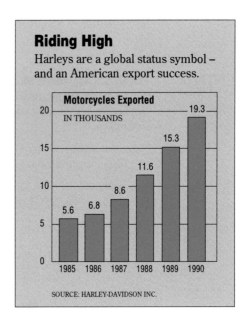

Riding High
Harleys are a global status symbol – and an American export success.

Motorcycles Exported
IN THOUSANDS

SOURCE: HARLEY-DAVIDSON INC.

Now listen to the extract and identify the mistake that Harley-Davidson made before 1981.

Franchising

KEY VOCABULARY

Franchising can be defined as a business system in which a company (or **franchisor**) sells an individual (or **franchisee**) the right to operate a business using the franchisor's established system or **format**. The franchisee is thus able to take advantage of the franchisor's brand names, reputation and experience.

As part of the contract (or **franchise agreement**) the franchisee pays an initial sum of money, known as a **franchise** (or **front end**) **fee**, to the franchisor and, in addition, agrees to pay a **management services fee**, which is usually calculated as a percentage of the annual turnover. In certain cases the franchisee may also pay an **advertising fee** to contribute to the franchisor's annual advertising and marketing costs. It is important to realise that the franchisee also has to put up the necessary capital to open the business.

Once the contract has been agreed, the franchisor provides an **operations manual** which is a document containing all the information that the franchisee requires in order to manage his or her business.

LEAD-IN

1 In pairs find as many examples as you can of franchise operations in your country in the following sectors.

Fast food	**Clothing**	**Car maintenance**
Burger King	*Tie Rack*	*Kwik Fit*
....	....	....
....	....	....
....	....	....
....	....	....

2 Read the following statements and decide which refer to franchisors (F'R) and which to franchisees (F'E).

	F'R	F'E
1 They can easily get advice on how to deal with specific problems.		
2 They do not have to borrow large amounts of capital to expand.		
3 They must respect certain rules.		
4 They may have to buy supplies from one source.		
5 They are responsible for national advertising.		
6 They can only sell certain products.		
7 They may not be able to sell the business easily.		
8 They provide regular reports on the level of sales.		
9 They can develop their business without having to deal with problems of recruiting and managing personnel.		

3 You will now hear Tony Dutfield, director of The British Franchise Association, talking about the franchise industry. Listen and complete the following chart.

Percentage success rate for franchises:		
Number of people employed:	USA	
	UK	
Annual turnover:	USA	
	UK	

READING

1 According to the text on the opposite page, are the following statements true or false?

	T	F
1 In most European countries franchised operations account for one tenth of the volume of retail business.		
2 The Blenheim group was responsible for the Paris Franchise show.		
3 According to some people, by the year 2000 fifty per cent of all the goods bought from shops in Europe will be from franchises.		
4 For companies who want to expand into foreign markets, setting up a franchise is the safest and most profitable way.		
5 US franchisors are planning to invest mainly in the UK.		
6 It is difficult for franchisors to obtain professional advice about how best to export their businesses.		
7 With the unified market it is safe to assume that what sells well in one European country will also sell well in another.		
8 Domino's Pizza was the first American food franchise to expand into Europe.		

Franchising makes sense for firms who find that local businessmen know best how to exploit their areas, writes **Iain McKelvie**

Massive growth in franchising across Europe is forecast over the next few years as trade barriers disappear.

Something of a boom is predicted by a number of companies who are preparing an onslaught on European markets which are still relatively underdeveloped in franchising.

France and Britain are the most franchised-developed countries, but even in these two it is reckoned that only ten per cent of retail sales are made through franchised outlets.

The most optimistic projections suggest that by the end of this decade as much as half of all sales in Europe will come through franchised outlets. American companies especially see Europe as a happy hunting ground and are using Britain with its common language as the launch pad for European expansion.

Names like McDonald's, Burger King, Kentucky Fried Chicken and, more recently, Domino's Pizza have already blazed trails across Europe. From now on it is likely to be US retailing and service companies that will make up the invasion force.

'We know of a number of US operators looking to use the UK as a foothold for moving into Europe,' says Stuart Brown a consultant with Stoy Hayward Franchising Services. 'We expect considerable growth in cross-border franchising as a means of achieving international development. In most cases, companies need a local partner who knows the market place. Hence the expansion through master licences of franchising. Joint ventures are the name of the game.'

In retailing, Body Shop has led the way in franchising in Europe. Having opened its first shop in Belgium in 1978 it now has more than 250 outlets in mainland Europe, from Finland to Portugal. Chairman Anita Roddick and her vision of local partnerships in other countries has made Body Shop one of the greatest retail successes since the war.

Benetton of Italy used the method of granting master licences to similar effect and another Italian casual clothing company, Stefanel, is using franchising to move into eastern European countries such as Czechoslovakia, Hungary, and Yugoslavia.

Local market expertise is essential, and while it means lower financial returns for the franchisor, the franchise method ensures lower risks.

Retailing is likely to be the biggest cross-border growth area and names like Mothercare, Evans (part of the Burton Group) and even Marks and Spencer are taking the franchise route to Europe. Next will come service companies, whether it be office cleaning, car tuning, computer technology, picture framing, hairdressing or legal services. One already making a move is Servicemaster, the US-based cleaning operator.

It is now well established in the UK and has moved into Germany, from where it is expecting to expand into other countries.

Printing services are another growth area. The US Kwik-Copy Corp is already well established in the UK under the name of Kall-Kwik, while the rival Sir Speedy has formed a joint venture with Fasprint de España with the aim of opening 200 print centres throughout mainland Europe in the next ten years through franchising.

To bring franchising to a wider public an increasing number of exhibitions are being held. The Blenheim Group are responsible for a number of these shows and their spokeswoman Cheryl Wallis says: 'Cross-border franchising is on the up and up now that trade restrictions are disappearing. Our Paris show was particularly well received. We had 22,000 visitors and 170 exhibitors, 12 per cent of whom were from outside France.' A number of French companies are poised to invade the UK via the franchise route, according to Peter Stern, senior franchise manager of NatWest. He says children's clothes retailer Jacadi, fashion chain Rodier, car-wash operator L'Elephant Bleu and three hoteliers are on the brink of franchising their business across the channel.

Blazing a trail across Europe

John Gooderham runs FMM Consultants International, which specialises in helping franchisors to expand out of the UK to all parts of the world. With associate companies in Paris, Cologne, Berlin, Milan and Amsterdam, FMM says cross-border franchising is flourishing. 'There may be no boundaries in Europe any more, but cultures remain very different.

'It is no use saying: what's good enough for the British is good enough for the French. You have to understand local culture, which is why franchising to local businessmen is the best way to expand.'

The range of franchise opportunities is now myriad. Nevada Bobs, a huge US golfing retailer, has opened six stores in the UK and is about to move onto the fairways of Germany and France.

Cross-border franchising is definitely the name of the game from now on.

BUSINESS FORMAT FRANCHISING 1990			
	Number of Franchises	Number of Franchise Outlets	Sales Franchises Billion ECU
AUSTRIA	53	1,583	-
BELGIUM	90	3,200	3.3
DENMARK	55	500	0.5
FRANCE	675	33,000	21.0
GERMANY	260	12,500	6.5
REP. IRELAND	20	-	0.1
ITALY	266	12,900	4.2
NETHERLANDS	302	10,200	6.2
NORWAY	120	850	0.5
PORTUGAL	50	800	-
SPAIN	117	14,500	2.1
SWEDEN	60	1,000	0.5
UK	379	18,260	7.5

The European

2 Read the article again and complete the following table.

Company	Country of origin	Sector	Markets Present	Future
Burger King	*USA*	*Fast Food*	*Europe*	—
		Children's Clothing		*UK*
Stefanel			*Italy*	
	USA		*UK Germany*	
Nevada Bobs	*USA*		*UK*	
	UK	*Body care*		—

3 Using the chart which accompanies the article calculate which of the following countries has the highest number of outlets per franchisor.

- Spain
- France
- Sweden
- Italy

VOCABULARY

1 Match the words from the text with their corresponding definitions.

1 boom (*line 5*)   **a** special skill or knowledge

2 outlet (*line 14*)   **b** money made on an investment

3 expect (*line 35*)   **c** to succeed in getting something

4 achieve (*line 37*)   **d** a big increase in business activity

5 licence (*line 41*)   **e** a shop that sells products made by a particular company

6 method (*line 52*)   **f** to control or be in charge of (an organisation)

7 expertise (*line 59*)   **g** a company or person who is competing against you

8 return (*line 60*)   **h** a document giving permission to make or sell something

9 rival (*line 80*)   **i** to think that something will happen

10 run (*line 111*)   **j** a way of doing something

2 Look at the following words from the text and complete the table.

Verb	Noun
expand	*expansion*
....	growth
....	success
predict	....
forecast	....
....	exhibition
....	consultant
establish	....
....	operator

3 A UK franchisor describes how his business has evolved. Complete his account using words from exercises 1 and 2. Change the form of the words where necessary.

We negotiated our first franchise in 1984 with a young couple, Brian and Anne Webster, who opened a(n) [1]............................. in Cambridge which they still [2]............................. today. Following the success of this operation we contacted a franchise [3]............................. who was able to help us to select ten additional franchisees who then set up their businesses in some of the major towns in the South of England. Since then our company has continued to [4]............................. and today we are [5]............................. in more than 50 locations across the country. This year, for the first time, we attended the two European franchise [6]............................. in Utrecht and Paris, where we had some very promising interviews with local [7]............................. who were interested in taking out a [8]............................. for our master franchise. We have [9]............................. that by 1996 we will have a total of 120 shops across Europe and almost all of these will be owned by franchisees.

DISCUSSION

1 Below you will find two advertisements for Uniglobe Travel franchises. Working in pairs, study them carefully. What are the differences between them? Where do you think they were published? What type of person is each one trying to attract? Discuss your conclusions with the pair next to you.

2 The Italian company Benetton is currently one of the most successful European franchisors. Founded in 1965 in Northern Italy by four members of the Benetton family, it was already selling its casual clothing in 5,900 shops in 82 different countries by 1990.

Like most franchisors, Benetton looks after national and international advertising for its franchisees. Recent Benetton advertising campaigns have been highly successful but also extremely controversial and have even been banned in some countries.

Working in pairs, discuss your reactions to the following Benetton advertisement. Does it shock you in any way? Why have people reacted to it so violently? What are the advantages and disadvantages of using such advertising?

LANGUAGE FOCUS

RELATIVE CLAUSES

Look at the following sentences from the text. The relative clause is in bold:

In most cases, companies need a local partner **who knows the market place**. (line 48)
John Gooderham runs FMM Consultants International, **which specialises in helping franchisors to expand out of the UK**. (line 111)

The relative clause in the first sentence is a **defining** clause. It tells us what type of partner is needed and is therefore essential to the meaning of the sentence. Companies wishing to expand into Europe do not need just any type of local partner, they need a special type: one who knows the market place.

The relative clause in the second sentence is a **non-defining** clause. It gives us extra information about FMM Consultants. This information is not needed to identify what is being talked about.

➤➤ The two types of clause are different in terms of grammar and punctuation. For more information, turn to page 155.

Practice

1 Look at the following sentences and decide whether they are defining (D) or non-defining (N) relative clauses.

	D	N
1 The design that we selected was in fact the most expensive.		
2 Wayne Calloway, who is from our Glasgow office, will be presenting the new project.		
3 The new investment plan, which was announced on Wednesday, will take five years to complete.		
4 The manager who made the mistake lost his job.		
5 This is Jane Stewart, whose company manufactures computer software.		
6 Paul Burrows? Is he the one whose office is next to Ian's?		

2 Join each pair of sentences using a relative pronoun.

Example:

> We signed an agreement. It will give us exclusive rights to several products.
> *The agreement which we signed will give us exclusive rights to several products.*

1 A woman introduced me to Mr Ross. She was Australian.

   The woman ....

2 I left a report on your desk last night. Have you read it?

   Have you ....?

3 We interviewed some people. They were very highly qualified.

   The people ....

4 You borrowed a man's car. What's his name?

   What's the name ....?

5 We use videos for training purposes. This is one of them.

   This is one of ....

From which of your sentences could the relative pronoun be omitted?

3 Choose the clause which best completes each of the seven sentences below.

> **a** whose engineers are among the most brilliant in the country
> **b** which cost the company over £1 million
> **c** whose salaries had not been increased
> **d** who was elected to the Board in 1984
> **e** which was written by our Marketing Manager
> **f** which has recently signed a contract with a Polish manufacturer
> **g** who is a specialist in Japanese management techniques

1 The firm's 300 employees, ..., went on strike.

2 The report, ..., contained many interesting ideas on how to promote our new products.

3 The firm, ..., intends to expand its presence in Eastern Europe.

4 The new machinery, ..., is not as efficient as we had hoped.

5 Mr Watanabe, ..., will be the main speaker at this year's conference.

6 KBJ Optics, ..., has over a hundred patented products.

7 The Chairman, ..., maintains close relations with the company's major investors.

SKILLS FOCUS

LISTENING

1 You will hear an interview with three executives involved in franchising, which was recorded at the Paris Franchise Exhibition. Listen and complete the following table.

Name	Position	Company name	Sector of activity	Number of outlets
John Hayes	—			—
Kay Ainsley			*Fast food*	
Klaus Ueber			*Cosmetics Toiletries*	

2 Study the following list of conditions that a franchisor might impose on a franchisee. Then listen to John Hayes and tick (✓) the ones he actually mentions.

☐ what bank to deal with

☐ how employees should be dressed

☐ what experience employees should have

☐ which computers to use

☐ how many hours a day a shop should operate

☐ how much to charge customers

☐ when to close the business for a holiday

☐ what to sell in the shop

☐ where to buy supplies

☐ how to talk to customers

3 You will now hear a dialogue in which Peter Stern, Senior Franchise Manager for the National Westminster Bank, answers the question: 'What kind of person makes a good franchisee?'

1 Listen and answer the questions below.

   a According to Peter Stern, why might a shy person not be a good franchisee?
   b What two questions does Peter Stern always ask potential franchisees?
   c What will a franchisor expect a franchisee to do?
   d What will a franchisee expect a franchisor to do?

2 Listen again and rewrite the following sentences by replacing the words in italics with those that the speaker actually uses.

   a A franchisee will be *working* with the *public* …
   b Successful franchisees *are generally* positive, outgoing *entrepreneurs* …
   c It's the *foundation* for a *good* relationship, that mutual relationship, and the fulfilment of both *parties* carrying out their *duties*.

SPEAKING

Study the vocabulary below which will help you to do the activities that follow.

Liquid capital: the amount of money that a franchisee must have available before a bank will be prepared to lend additional capital. Also known as ready cash.

Working capital: the money that a franchisee will use to buy the stock and to pay for the labour and services that the business will need.

On-going fees: the various payments that the franchisee makes to the franchisor for the assistance and services he or she provides.

1 Work in pairs. Student A should look at the information below, and Student B at the information on page 148.

Student A

You are interested in taking out a franchise with Perfect Pizza. You have seen the following advertisement and decide to call Martin Clayton, Franchise Sales Director for Perfect Pizza (played by Student B). Ask questions and complete the notes.

Examples: *How much liquid capital is required to set up an outlet?*
What is the initial franchise fee?

Last year we sold six million pizzas and we're still hungry.

PERFECT PIZZA
FREE DELIVERY

If you want to join one of the fastest growing companies in fast food, we can offer:

■ market leadership and a proven track record
■ one of the industry's fastest paybacks
■ national and local marketing
■ the back up, training and operational expertise of a professional franchise team
■ the advantages of central buying and distribution of quality products

Call Martin Clayton now on 0932 568000.

Liquid capital requirement: ....

Working capital requirement: ....

Initial franchise fee: ....

On-going fees: ....

....

Projected turnover of typical outlet:

....

....

....

Projected profit of typical outlet:

....

....

....

Year company established: ....

Number of outlets: ....

Regions available: ....

Length of contract: ....

You should now play the role of Bernard Glover, Franchise Development Manager for Budget Rent a Car. Student B is interested in taking out a franchise with you. Look at the information on the following page and answer his or her questions.

Budget Rent a Car

**Budget Rent a Car International Inc.,
41 Marlowes, Hemel Hempstead,
Herts. HP1 1LD.
Tel. 0442 218027
Fax. 0442 230757**

Type of business: vehicle rental
Applications invited: yes
Availability: North-West England and Scotland
Company established: 1966
Number of outlets in the UK: company owned 41,
franchised 119
Number of outlets worldwide: 3,300
Working capital: £50,000
Liquid capital requirement: £75,000
Initial franchise fee: £25,000
On-going fees: management services fee 7½%,
marketing/advertising levy: 2½%
Typical outlet, projected turnover:
year 1 - £150,000, year 2 - £240,000,
year 3 - £300,000
Typical outlet, projected profit/(loss):
year 1 – (£20,000), year 2 – break-even,
year 3 – £10,000-£20,000
Period of contract: 5 years
BFA membership: full

2 Working in the same pairs, discuss the main differences between the two franchises.

WRITING   You have been asked to prepare a short report summarising some of the main characteristics of the UK franchise market. Use the information in the charts below to prepare your summary.

3   % of Total Turnover by Regions

1   Employment

2   Motivation (why people choose franchising)

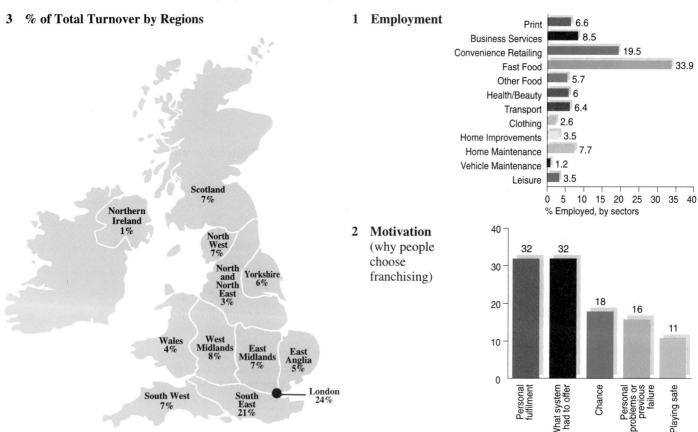

Japan and the Business World

LEAD-IN

1 It is a well known fact that Japan holds a top economic position in the world today. In groups, read the following statements and discuss how they might influence the performance of Japanese business in the years to come. Present your views to the class.

- Japan will have the most aged population of all industrial countries by 2010.
- The rest of the world owes Japan over $400 billion.
- Japanese companies employ 68% of the world's robots.
- In 1990, Japan held one third of the US automobile market.
- Eight of the world's ten biggest banks are Japanese.
- By the year 2000, 16% of British factories will be run by Japanese bosses.
- Between 1988 and 1989, the number of European companies bought by Japanese companies practically doubled.
- There is a very serious lack of workers entering the workforce in Japan.
- Japanese investors do up to 25% of the buying and selling on the New York Stock Exchange.

2 In the OECD (Organisation for Economic Co-operation and Development), Japan is the country with the longest working week (46.8 hours). Using the list of countries below and any knowledge you have of them, try to identify the average number of hours worked per week in each.

1	Portugal	**a**	34.3 hours
2	United States	**b**	37.2 hours
3	France	**c**	38.9 hours
4	Netherlands	**d**	39.5 hours
5	Spain	**e**	40.3 hours
6	United Kingdom	**f**	43 hours

Source: OECD

After your teacher has given you the correct answers, discuss what you think could be the consequences of working 46.8 hours a week.

READING

1 You are going to read an article about a Japanese phenomenon known as *karoshi*. Before you read the article properly, look through it quickly to find out what *karoshi* means.

DATELINE

DYING TO WORK

¹ **TOKYO** – A recent television special said it all: It showed a building in downtown Tokyo with preprogrammed office lights that uniformly shut off at 10 p.m.; seconds later, virtually every light in the building came right back on. Despite such displays, the nation that has taken the sting out of the word 'workaholic,' ⁵ producing 10 percent of the world's exports with just 2 percent of its population, is suddenly obsessed with a deadly phenomenon known as *karoshi*. That's the Japanese word for 'death from overwork.' Tetsunojo Uehata, the medical authority who coined the word, defines *karoshi* as a 'condition in which psychologically unsound work processes are allowed to continue in a way that disrupts the ¹⁰ worker's normal work and life rhythms, leading to a buildup of fatigue in the body and a chronic condition of overwork accompanied by a worsening of pre-existent high blood pressure and a ¹⁵ hardening of the arteries and finally resulting in a fatal breakdown.' Translation: All work and no play can really wreck one's health, even in ²⁰ Japan.

Stressed. *At work in Japan*

Hardly a week goes by without a grim report about some overzealous worker in the prime of his life who could ²⁵ not just say no to overtime. Not long ago, a 39-year-old police sergeant, Haruo Okada, captured headlines as a *karoshi* victim by working double shifts for a month during the enthronement ceremonies for the nation's new monarch. There are no reliable figures on the number of victims, but analysts ³⁰ believe that tens of thousands of Japanese become seriously ill or die from overwork each year. Despite promises by the government to trim working hours, the average Japanese clocked 2,150 hours in 1989, compared with 1,924 hours for Americans and 1,643 hours for the French.

Some Japanese want change. When a group of lawyers and doctors set up the ³⁵ nation's first *karoshi* hot line in 1988, 135 people phoned in on the first day. Since then, nearly 2,000 cases have been reported to the 42 hot lines across the nation, and an international call-in center has been set up recently.

To raise public awareness about the problem and to pressure the government and corporate Japan into action, a group of lawyers, doctors and victims' wives has ⁴⁰ published a book called '*Karoshi:* When the Corporate Warrior Dies,' which recounts numerous horror stories. Yet the government and most Japanese companies rarely acknowledge *karoshi* and provide no special compensation to survivors. As the Ministry of Labour defines it, overwork can only be considered a cause of death if a victim 'worked continuously for 24 hours preceding death,' or ⁴⁵ 'worked 16 hours a day for seven consecutive days leading up to death.'

Alas, the recent media attention probably won't slow down the production lines much. In a poll conducted by an insurance company, more than 40 percent of the employees the firm covered said they feared that overwork might kill them; few planned to do anything about it. All in all, it looks like another busy year for the ⁵⁰ folks at the *karoshi* hot line.

By Jim Impoco

US News & World Report

2 Now read the text in more detail and decide if the following statements are true or false?

	T	F

1   Japan has a relatively small population, but is a major world exporter.

2   The Ministry of Labour knows the exact number of *karoshi* victims.

3   People can call special telephone numbers to report cases of death from overwork.

4   A book has been written to inform the public about the *karoshi* problem, and to make the government and companies react.

5   The Japanese government and many companies usually admit that there is a problem with overwork.

6   Many of the employees recently questioned by an insurance company said that they are trying to change their working habits.

VOCABULARY

Rewrite the sentences below, replacing the words and phrases in italics with the following words from the text.

authority (*line 7*)   figures (*line 29*)
overtime (*line 25*)   compensation (*line 42*)
headline (*line 27*)   production (*line 46*)
shifts (*line 28*)   poll (*line 47*)

1   John received *payment* from his company after injuring himself at work.

2   The factory has two *periods of working time*: 8 a.m. to 4 p.m. and 4 p.m. to midnight.

3   Tom Peters is a world famous *expert* on management problems.

4   The *title* on the front page of today's newspaper is 'Priceless painting stolen from Washington museum'.

5   We have just received the sales *statistics* for the Far East.

6   I'm going to have to put in a lot of *extra hours* this week.

7   By modernizing its factories, the firm hopes to increase its *output*.

8   We carried out a *survey of public opinion* to find out what young consumers thought about the two different brands of soft drink.

DISCUSSION

1 Read the following observation made by a Japanese executive:

For the Japanese, hard work is a pleasure and a personal achievement. It is the result of a long tradition. Working makes one noble and for the Japanese, it is the duty to one's company that counts.

Does the attitude towards work in your country correspond to the one you have just read? Do people generally have a strong feeling of loyalty towards the company they work for? What is the attitude to overtime?

2 Japanese workers are entitled to two weeks' holiday per year, but many of them take only one week off. This situation, however, is starting to change slowly. People are determined to enjoy life more and are spending more money on leisure. Some companies are granting longer holiday time to their workers and in a recent survey 80% of university graduates said that a five-day working week was a major requirement when choosing a job.

In your opinion, are holiday and leisure time important aspects of a person's working life?

LANGUAGE FOCUS

EXPRESSING CONTRAST

Look at the following sentences from the text:

Despite such displays, the nation that has taken the sting out of the word 'workaholic' ... is suddenly obsessed with a deadly phenomenon known as karoshi. (para. 1)

This sentence means that the Japanese are still working very hard, but they have become worried about the *karoshi* phenomenon.

Despite promises by the government to trim working hours, the average Japanese clocked 2,150 hours in 1989 .... (para. 2)

This sentence means that the Japanese government has promised to reduce working hours, but the Japanese still continue to work very hard.

You will notice that, in each sentence, the word *despite* is used to express a contrast between two ideas. What other ways of expressing contrast can you think of?

➤➤ For more information, turn to page 155.

Practice

Finish each of the following sentences so that it has the same meaning as the sentence printed before it.

Example:
Although he is intelligent, he does not find solutions to production problems very easily.
In spite of his intelligence, he does not find solutions to production problems very easily.

1 Although some Japanese women are successful in business, the majority of Japanese companies are run by men.

In spite of ....
....

2 In spite of their dedication to their companies, many young Japanese employees want more leisure time.

Although ....
....

3 Although they have intense work habits, many Japanese socialise quite easily after work.

Despite ....
....

4 Despite the increase in their salaries, 60 per cent of Japanese workers still spend Saturday at work.

Even though ....
....

5 Although some Japanese and American management practices are similar, there are many striking differences between them.

Despite ....
....

6 The headquarters of most major Japanese companies are located in Tokyo despite the very expensive rents.

The headquarters of most major Japanese companies are located in Tokyo, even though

....

SKILLS FOCUS

MEMO WRITING

A **memorandum** (or memo) is a very common form of business communication. It is a relatively informal written document which is exchanged between members of the same organisation. The memo usually focuses on one message or piece of information, and often requests action to be taken.

There are many different techniques used in memo writing, but several basic rules should always be applied:

- Since memos are rather informal documents, it is best to use simple language and a conversational tone.
- Keep your memo clear. Use short, simple sentences.
- A memo should not be longer than one page. Most people do not have time to read long memos.

Look at this memo, then match each numbered section to the labels which follow.

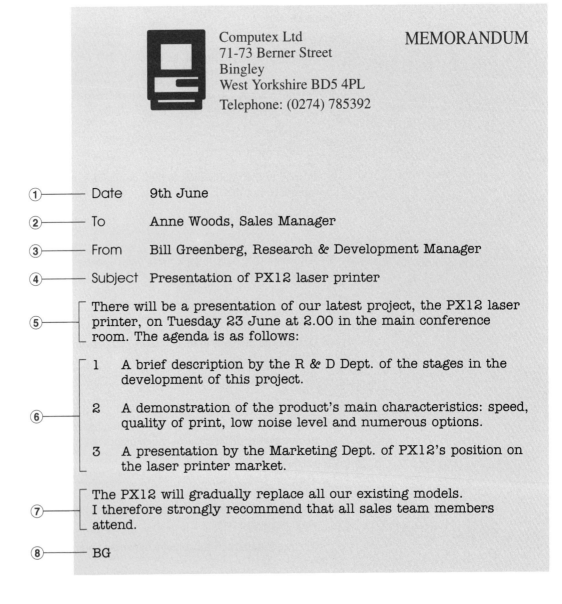

Computex Ltd
71-73 Berner Street
Bingley
West Yorkshire BD5 4PL
Telephone: (0274) 785392

MEMORANDUM

1. Date   9th June

2. To   Anne Woods, Sales Manager

3. From   Bill Greenberg, Research & Development Manager

4. Subject   Presentation of PX12 laser printer

5. There will be a presentation of our latest project, the PX12 laser printer, on Tuesday 23 June at 2.00 in the main conference room. The agenda is as follows:

6.
1   A brief description by the R & D Dept. of the stages in the development of this project.

2   A demonstration of the product's main characteristics: speed, quality of print, low noise level and numerous options.

3   A presentation by the Marketing Dept. of PX12's position on the laser printer market.

7. The PX12 will gradually replace all our existing models. I therefore strongly recommend that all sales team members attend.

8. BG

○ The 'body' of the memo, usually divided into numbered paragraphs which develop the information.

○ A short heading, which tells you what the memo is about.

① Date on which the memo is sent.

○ The conclusion of the memo, which often recommends a course of action.

○ Name of the person sending the memo.

○ Unlike letters, the memo does not contain forms of address (such as Dear Ms X) or the sender's signature. The sender usually types his or her name or initials at the end of the memo.

○ Name of the person to whom the memo is sent.

○ A brief introduction to the memo giving the most important information.

Now do the listening activity in preparation for writing your own memo.

LISTENING 1   Philip Groves, Managing Director of a European pharmaceutical company, will soon be sending a delegation of executives to Japan for the first time to negotiate an important contract. Since he wants the negotiations to go smoothly, he thinks it would be a good idea for the executives to attend a series of seminars on Japanese culture and management given by Tomomi Moriwake, a Japanese consultant. He has asked Vincent Mills, the Human Resources Manager, to talk to Ms Moriwake in order to find out more about the content of her seminars. He has also requested that Mr Mills send him a memo summarising his conversation with Ms Moriwake and recommending a course of action.

1 You will hear the Japanese consultant discussing the content of her seminars. Listen and take as many notes as you can under the following headings. These notes will help you to organise the memo which you will be writing later on.

Emphasis on the group	Human relationships	Japanese managers

2 Compare your notes with those of your partner. Did your partner hear any information that you missed? Listen again and finalise your notes.

WRITING   Read the instructions for writing a memo again and look at the model provided. Working on your own or with your partner, you should now write the memo that Vincent Mills will send to his Managing Director. Be sure to respect the standard memo format and do not forget to include the course of action that Mr Mills thinks should be taken.

LISTENING 2

The same Japanese consultant gives a number of tips, or recommendations, for doing business with the Japanese. She talks about the four topics shown in the chart below.

1 Listen and complete the chart with the recommendations she makes and the reasons she gives for each. The first part of the chart has been filled in for you.

Tips for doing business with the Japanese

Topic	Recommendation	Reason(s)
Age of executives	Young men should not be sent to conduct business negotiations in Japan.	• Seniority is important in lifetime employment system. • Japanese top executives are much older than American ones. • It is an insult to the Japanese to do business with young people.
The business card		
Socialising		
Business meetings and negotiations		

2 Discuss the following questions in groups.

1 Could any of the recommendations for doing business in Japan that you have just heard also apply to your country? Which ones?

2 What is the average age of senior executives in your country? Do young people and women play an active role in business?

Business and the Environment

LEAD-IN   **1** In groups, discuss the following cartoons and decide which major environmental threats they refer to. Find out which cartoon the group considers to be the most effective and which environmental causes it thinks are the most important today. Present your findings to the class.

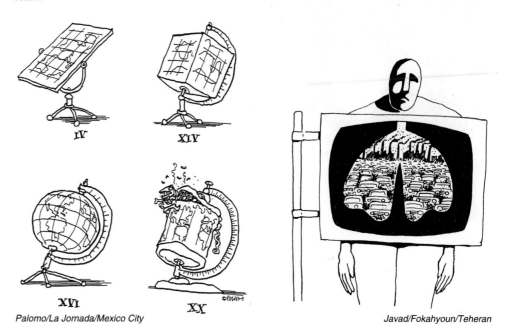

IV   XIV

XVI   XX

Palomo/La Jornada/Mexico City

Javad/Fokahyoun/Teheran

Ewk/Aftonbladet/Stockholm

Cummings/Free Press/Winnipeg

2 Here are some statements about the role of business in environmental affairs. Discuss which ones you agree with and why.

'A good business should be part of society, and you should lead by example. You have to have pride in what you do. There's no pride in making millions of pounds, but there is pride in helping people and the environment.'

'The idea now is global responsibility. Businesses are the true planetary citizens, they can push frontiers, they can change society.'

'In the 90s, environmentalism will be the most important issue for business.'

READING

The statements you have just read were made by Anita Roddick, founder and managing director of The Body Shop International. The first branch of The Body Shop was opened in Brighton (UK) in 1976 and the company now trades in 40 countries, more than any other British retailer. The Body Shop is against using animals in testing cosmetics and is very active in community projects. It is particularly well known for its involvement in environmental causes, some of which are described in the text opposite.

Read the text and answer the following questions.

1 What are the differences between the two demonstrations mentioned in the text? Why in your opinion did one of these demonstrations attract more attention?

2 According to the text, why aren't people in the UK surprised by The Body Shop's activism?

3 How does the Trade Not Aid program help developing countries?

4 According to Anita Roddick, what kind of publicity best increases sales of her products?

5 What effect do Anita Roddick's environmental policies have on (a) her workforce and (b) sales and profits? How are these two linked?

VOCABULARY

1 Use the following words from the text to complete the passage below. Use the plural form where necessary.

campaign (*line 14*)	fund-raising (*line 19*)	publicity (*line 61*)
mobilise (*line 18*)	display (*line 20*)	audience (*line 69*)
petition (*line 18*)	issue (*line 22*)	

The Body Shop believes that people should be aware of today's major environmental and social ¹............................. That is why they frequently organise ²............................. to draw the public's attention to serious problems, such as the protection of endangered animals or the imprisonment of political dissidents. Thanks to The Body Shop's strong educational policy for staff members, individual shops play an active role in ³............................. support for these various causes. For example, almost one million people signed The Body Shop's ⁴............................. against the burning of the Brazilian rainforest in a two-week campaign. Shops also organise ⁵............................. events to obtain money for important causes, and fact sheets, leaflets and window ⁶............................. ensure that people all over the world (customers and staff alike) get the message. The Body Shop's prominent position on the High Street gives their activities a wide ⁷............................., and the ⁸............................. they receive through the press contributes to extending their message still further into the community.

A BANNER OF VALUES
Creating a global community

On a cold night in January, a ragtag group of environmentalists gathers outside the Brazilian embassy in London. There are about 20 of them, the usual suspects, from such organisations as Friends of the Earth and Survival International.
5 They have come to draw attention to the plight of the Yanomami Indians, a Stone Age tribe that is being wiped out by diseases brought to its remote Brazilian habitat by miners looking for gold. At the moment, however, there is not much attention to be drawn. Aside from an occasional passing taxi,
10 the only people around are the protesters. Among them is Anita Roddick, founder and managing director of The Body Shop International.

She is there, moreover, in her official capacity. Recently her company has engaged in a worldwide campaign that has
15 drawn much attention to the plight of all the inhabitants of the Amazon rain forest. The Body Shop and its franchisees have contributed hundreds of thousands of dollars to their defense. It has mobilised employees for petition drives and fund-raising campaigns, carried out through the stores and
20 on company time. It has produced window displays, posters, T-shirts, brochures, and videotapes to educate people about the issues. It has brought 250 employees to London for a major demonstration at this very embassy – not on a dark night, but in broad daylight, with a television crew broadcasting the event
25 live, via satellite, to Brazil.

In the United States such corporate activism would be considered bizarre, if not dangerously radical. In the United Kingdom it draws attention, but it no longer generates much surprise. That's mainly because The Body Shop has been
30 acting this way for years. Long before it launched its rain-forest offensive, after all, it waged similar campaigns against everything from the killing of whales to the repression of political dissidents. Almost as well known, and accepted, are its efforts to help communities in developing countries by
35 setting them up as suppliers under a program it calls Trade Not Aid. Then there's the soap factory it has built in a poverty-stricken section of Glasgow, Scotland with the explicit (and well-publicised) purpose of providing jobs for people who, in some cases, have been unemployed for
40 upward of 10 years. Not to mention the community project that every shop is required to have and that every shop employee is expected to work in for at least one hour a week – a paid hour, that is, on company time.

Indeed, there is almost no end to the list of such Body
45 Shop activities, most of which have been widely reported in the British press. This inevitably raises a question in the minds of many people, one Anita almost always hears when she appears before business groups. "They want to know, 'Isn't it all public relations? Aren't you just using these cam-
50 paigns and activities to create more sales and profits?"

On the campaign trail

She bristles at the question. "Look," she says, "if I put our poster for Colourings (a line of makeup) in the shop windows, that creates sales and profits. A poster to stop the burning of the rain forest doesn't. It creates a banner of
55 values, it links us to the community, but it will not increase sales. What increases sales is an article in boring Glamour magazine saying Princess Diana uses Body Shop products. Then we'll get 7,000 bloody phone calls asking for our catalog. You can measure the effect".

60 It's a provocative argument, but it's a little misleading. Most of the activities are, in fact, intended to generate publicity for The Body Shop, and the company milks them for all they're worth. Even Anita would admit, moreover, that – over the long term – they do tend to increase sales and, yes,
65 profits. What's most interesting, however, is the way that happens. Indeed, this may be the single most striking aspect of The Body Shop's entire approach to business.

The first thing you have to understand is that the primary audience for these activities is not the public: it is her
70 own work force. The campaigns, which play a major role in her educational program, are anything but random attempts to promote goodwill. They are part of a carefully researched, designed, and executed business strategy.

She wants causes that will generate real excitement and
75 enthusiasm in the shops. "You educate people by their passions, especially young people," she says. "You find ways to grab their imagination. You want them to feel that they're doing something important, that they're not a lone voice, that they are the most powerful, potent people on the planet."

INC.

2 Match the nouns to the verbs with which they are commonly used. The answers can be found in the text.

1	to play	**a**	a question (about sth)
2	to draw	**b**	a campaign (against sth)
3	to raise	**c**	attention (to sth)
4	to grab	**d**	a major role (in sth)
5	to wage	**e**	someone's imagination

3 Use the expressions from exercise 2 to replace the words in italics in the following sentences. You will need to change the form of some of the words.

1 The government is *fighting against* all forms of discrimination.
2 Her plans *excited and inspired* the entire company.
3 I would like to *point out* the following facts.
4 Money *was an important factor in* my decision to accept the job.
5 The report *expresses doubts about* his ability to do the job.

4 Find words in the text which have the opposite meaning of those listed below.

1 accessible .... (*para. 1*)   **6** disconnects .... (*para. 5*)

2 local .... (*para. 2*)   **7** losses .... (*para. 5*)

3 attack .... (*para. 2-AmE*)   **8** deny .... (*para. 6*)

4 still .... (*para. 3*)   **9** precise .... (*para. 7*)

5 demolished .... (*para. 3*)   **10** boredom .... (*para. 8*)

The answer to number 3 is the American English spelling. What is the British English spelling?

DISCUSSION

1 What do you think of The Body Shop's approach to business?

2 How is 'corporate activism' seen in your country?

3 What examples are there in your country of companies that are doing something for the environment?

LANGUAGE FOCUS

THE PASSIVE   Look at the following sentences:

Anita Roddick opened the first branch of The Body Shop in 1976.
The first branch of The Body Shop was opened in 1976.

What are the differences between the two sentences in terms of (a) the information they contain, (b) emphasis, (c) the form of the verb?

➤➤ For information on the passive, turn to page 156.

Practice

1 The following diagram shows the different stages in the manufacture and recycling of The Body Shop bottle. Use the verbs below to complete each stage with a present simple form of the passive. The first stage has been done for you.

add	grind	remove
arrange	heat	return
extract	label	transport
fill	produce	use

THE STORY OF THE BODY SHOP BOTTLE

1 Oil _is extracted_ from beneath the sea. It contains hydrocarbons which _are used_ to produce plastic.

2 The plastic .... and injected into a mould to produce the bottle shape.

3 The bottles .... with different Body Shop products and .... to show what each one contains.

4 Caps .... to seal the bottles.

5 The bottles .... in packs and then .... to the shops by lorry.

6 Once empty, bottles .... to the shops, where the caps ....

7 The bottles and caps .... up into two separate types of plastic.

8 Items such as combs .... from the recovered plastic.

ONCE IS NOT ENOUGH

65

2 Change the following sentences into the passive. You should omit the agent if it is not important.

1 The Body Shop introduced peppermint foot lotion specially for the London Marathon.
2 The Soapworks factory will make new products in future.
3 The company can discontinue a product if it is not successful.
4 Detailed labels give information about how consumers should use the product.
5 Before The Body Shop entered the American market, it had already established a strong image in the UK.
6 The Body Shop has recently added more than 30 items to its product range.
7 The Body Shop does not test its products on animals.
8 Customers may return plastic bottles for refilling.

DESCRIBING GROUPS AND SUBGROUPS

Look at the following extract from the text:

On a cold night in January, a ragtag group of environmentalists gathers outside the Brazilian embassy in London. **There are about 20 of them***, the usual suspects, from such organizations as Friends of the Earth and Survival International.* (para. 1)

When we want to specify the total number of people or things in a group, we use *there are*.

There are *sixteen employees working in the marketing department.*

If we subdivide the group, we use an expression such as *some of, none of, all of, most of, one/two/three of.*

Five of them *are men.*

Practice

1 Look at the table which contains information about a company's marketing department and complete the description. Use the following words:

half	none	two	most	a few	all

Total number of employees	16
Part-time employees	0
Female employees	11
Male employees	5
Graduates	8
Trainees	2
Employees with computer skills	16
Employees with language skills	3

There are sixteen employees working in the marketing department, [1].............................. of whom are women. [2]............................ of them are part-time employees, [3]............................ of them are graduates and [4]............................ of them are trainees. [5]............................ of them have computer skills and [6]............................ of them can speak a foreign language.

2 Divide into groups of six and conduct a survey to find out how many people in the group have done the following:

■ bought a Body Shop product

■ watched a TV documentary on an environmental topic

■ taken something to be recycled

■ joined an environmental association

■ demonstrated for an environmental cause

Each group should now present a summary of their findings to the rest of the class. You should use the following structures in your presentations.

All of us …
Half of us …
Some/A few of us …
Two/three etc. of us …
None of us …

SKILLS FOCUS

SPEAKING

Environmental case studies

Throughout the world, consumers are becoming increasingly concerned about the effects of industry on the environment. As a result, many companies are now looking for ways to improve their existing products or to develop new 'environmentally friendly' products. The McDonald's Corporation, for instance, decided to replace the plastic foam packaging of its hamburgers with a new paper alternative, partly in response to pressure from consumers and environmental groups. It is also examining ways of reducing, reusing and recycling other packaging and shipping materials.

Each of the following cases deals with a product that has been or is criticised for its negative impact on the environment. In groups, read each case and discuss which solutions you think were found or are being studied by the company in order to improve or change the product. Present your findings to the class.

1 Procter and Gamble
When thrown away after use, the large 65-ounce plastic bottles of 'Downy' fabric softener created large quantities of solid waste and filled up local landfill sites.

2 General Motors
Carbon monoxide emissions from cars are responsible for air pollution, acid rain and the global warming of the planet.

3 Goodyear
Scrap tyres are piled up in landfill dumps and pollute the air when burned.

4 Kodak
The popular plastic single-use cameras were simply thrown away after the film was developed.

5 HJ Heinz
Dolphins were often killed in the nets used to catch tuna for its 'Starkist' brand of canned tuna.

6 Empire Berol USA
Rain forests in Indonesia were being destroyed to obtain the tropical hardwood jelutong used in the pencils manufactured by the company.

LISTENING

1 A customer survey

You will hear eight customers interviewed in a London Body Shop explaining why they buy Body Shop products and not similar products that are available in other shops. Listen, and complete the table below with the reason(s) each customer gives.

Customers	Reasons for buying Body Shop products
1	
2	
3 & 4	
5	
6	
7	
8	

2 You will now hear David Wheeler, Head of Environmental Affairs of The Body Shop. In the first extract, he explains why he believes companies will have to pay closer attention to environmental matters in the future. In the second extract, he discusses some of the measures being taken by The Body Shop as far as packaging is concerned. Take notes as you listen to the two extracts and then write a short summary (2 to 3 lines) for each in the spaces provided below.

Extract 1 – Summary:

....

....

....

Extract 2 – Summary:

....

....

....

WRITING

Look around your house or flat and choose *several different products* from the list below that you consume or use daily:

- food and beverages
- toiletries (soap, shampoo, etc.)
- detergents and cleaning products
- paper and paper products
- car or machine maintenance products
- plant and gardening products

After reading the labels and packaging of the products you have chosen, make a list of the words and expressions that describe the products' qualities from an environmental point of view (*natural, non-polluting,* etc.). In a short composition, explain whether your purchasing decisions are based on environmental concerns.

Retailing

KEY VOCABULARY

Retailing is the general term covering all forms of selling goods to the public. It is a profitable sector in the UK, especially for larger food retailers.

Retail businesses in the UK are usually classified according to the number of shops or outlets they have.

The smallest operations, such as local grocery or convenience stores are called **single outlet retailers**. These are independent businesses run from one shop.

Small multiple retailers operate a maximum of nine shops, all selling the same range of products.

Large multiple retailers (also known as **chain stores**) are the big names in the business, such as Marks and Spencer. These companies have large numbers of stores selling a wide variety of items. Some operate from out of town locations with parking facilities, known as either **superstores** (over 20,000 square feet) or **hypermarkets** (over 50,000 square feet).

Department stores, such as Harrods in London, are large shops which sell a wide variety of products. They are organised in departments, each with its own manager, and are usually found in city centres.

LEAD-IN

1 In pairs or small groups, discuss the retail business in your country. Who are the major retailers? Do they specialise in specific products or do they sell a wide variety of items? Present your findings to the class.

2 You will hear Dr Steve Burt of Stirling University describing some of the main differences between retailing in the UK and in continental Europe. Using the headings in the left-hand column, complete the table to show what these differences are.

	UK	Continental Europe
Pricing		
Margins* of food retailers		
Types of stores and products sold		
Management of retail businesses		

* The term margin refers to the percentage profit made on sales.

READING

Read the article on the opposite page about a hi-fi retailer called Richer Sounds and choose the best answer for each of the following questions.

1 Richer Sounds is
  a a single outlet retailer.
  b a privately-owned multiple.
  c a department store.

2 Richer Sounds
  a sells five times more than Marks and Spencer.
  b has more outlets than most UK retailers.
  c sells more per square foot than any other UK retailer.

3 Richer Sounds is cheaper than other hi-fi retailers because
  a it only sells old models of hi-fi equipment.
  b it buys equipment from manufacturers at special prices.
  c it sells second-hand equipment.

4 Manufacturers like doing business with Richer Sounds because
  a it can handle small numbers of items.
  b it has a major distribution network.
  c it accepts lower discounts than other retailers.

5 Richer Sounds
  a does all its advertising through brochures.
  b relies on getting free publicity from newspaper and magazine articles.
  c buys advertising space at a low price.

6 At Richer Sounds, staff
  a regularly receive further training.
  b are taught to sell aggressively.
  c install equipment for their customers.

Richer pickings

At hi-fi chain Richer Sounds 'we have a laugh', says founder Julian Richer. They also sell more per square foot than any retailer in Britain. By Nigel Cope.

Who is the busiest retailer in Britain? Marks & Spencer? Sainsbury perhaps, or Tesco? Wrong on all three counts. The answer is Richer Sounds, a little-known, privately owned, cut-price retailer of hi-fi equipment with 12 shops in the UK.

In this year's *Guinness Book of Records*, Richer Sounds warrants an entry for the highest sales per square foot of any retailer in the UK – £16,635 – for its store on London Bridge Walk in the City. Even taking an average across all 12 stores, Richer Sounds clocks up £2,500 per square foot, five times more than Marks & Spencer, treble the sales achieved by Sainsbury.

It is profitable too. Last year – the year of the dog for UK retailing – Richer Sounds made profits of more than £500,000 on sales of almost £12 million.

The man behind Richer Sounds' success is founder, managing director and 98 per cent shareholder Julian Richer, a 31-year-old Londoner who, at the age of 14, used to buy and sell candles during the energy crisis of 1974. A likeable bloke who wears his blond hair in a pony tail and operates from a small converted Victorian vinegar factory in Bermondsey, south-east London, he raps out his sales pitch.

"Even when I was at school I wanted to go into business," he says, "but my age was against me. Property was out – I wasn't old enough to sign a contract. Cars were out – I couldn't drive. So I turned to hi-fi, which was catching on at school. I bought a second-hand Bang & Olufsen for £10, did it up and sold it for £22." In 1979, at the age of 19, he opened his first shop – the one on London Bridge Walk.

Since then, little has changed. In simple terms, Richer Sounds sells discounted hi-fi from tiny, basic shops with low overheads. Stock turnover is rapid and the company's smallness gives it flexibility to take advantage of deals offered by manufacturers on end-of-line or surplus equipment.

The technique has enabled Richer Sounds to secure itself a lucrative niche in a £4 billion audio visual market dominated by independents.

While leading multiples stock mainly the mass market, volume selling midi systems which became popular in the early 1980s, Richer Sounds supplies only hi-fi separates such as turntables and amplifiers. It buys either end-of-line ranges which manufacturers are hoping to off-load before the next, cosmetically different, model arrives from Japan, or small orders of current models which, perhaps because of poor stock management, the manufacturer is prepared to sell at a reduced price. Now, as manufacturers' stock control improves, three-quarters of its stock is current models.

Suppliers are keen to do business with this quirky retailer. "People like Dixons and Comet have so many stores (900 and 300 respectively) that unless you've got 5,000 of a model it's not worth their while putting it into their distribution system," says Clive Roberts, sales and marketing director of Akai. "With Richer, you can do a deal on 30."

Marketing is a key weapon. Richer Sounds advertises regularly in national newspapers ("We buy late space at a discount," Richer says) and in alternative magazines such as *Private Eye* and *Viz*. Every month it produces 100,000 copies of a brochure pushing the latest offers.

The shops are like walk-in warehouses. Outside, "bargain bins" tout special offers including video tapes at 99p and cassettes for 69p. Inside, compact disc players, turntables and speakers from leading names such as Sony, Akai and Marantz are stacked from floor to ceiling. Banners hanging from the ceiling proclaim: "If you've seen it cheaper, we'll beat that price by £10."

Good service is another priority. At Richer Sounds staff are trained not to be pushy. They all attend two training seminars a year at Richer's country house in Yorkshire, where more attention is paid to following the correct administrative procedures.

First-time hi-fi buyers get a call to check that they have plugged in the equipment correctly. Customer receipts include a freephone number they can dial if they have a problem. Richer's own name and office number are supplied too.

The emphasis is on fun. If it is raining, customers are given a free umbrella. In summer they get a Chilly Willy (a type of ice lolly). Other seasonal gifts include mince pies at Christmas and hot-cross buns at Easter. "We have a laugh," Richer says. "We don't take ourselves seriously, but we do take our customers seriously."

Business

VOCABULARY

1 The following words can be used in more than one way. Look at how they are used in the text and underline the correct part of speech.

1 deal (*line 51*)   <u>noun</u>   verb

2 surplus (*line 52*)   noun   adjective

3 secure (*line 54*)   verb   adjective

4 stock (*line 57*)   noun   verb

5 model (*line 65*)   noun   verb   adjective

6 order (*line 66*)   noun   verb

7 stock (*line 72*)   noun   verb

Now discuss with a partner what the words mean in the context of the text.

2 Match the words on the left with the words on the right to make compound nouns.

Example: *compact disc*

1	compact	**a**	system
2	distribution	**b**	offer
3	mass	**c**	name
4	special	**d**	market
5	leading	**e**	pitch
6	sales	**f**	disc

3 Now match these words with their corresponding definitions.

1 retailer (*line 1*)   **a** reduction in the original price of a product

2 profit (*line 20*)   **b** the variety of products that a company makes or sells

3 overheads (*line 48*)   **c** a company which sells goods or equipment to another company

4 turnover (*line 48*)   **d** a building where goods are stored

5 range (*line 63*)   **e** the rate at which goods are sold

6 supplier (*line 73*)   **f** the expenses involved in running a business, such as rent, lighting and salaries

7 discount (*line 86*)   **g** a piece of paper which tells customers how much money they have paid for a product

8 warehouse (*line 91*)   **h** a person or shop that sells goods to the public

9 receipt (*line 112*)   **i** the amount of money which is made by a business, for example when it sells something for more than it cost

4 The passage below describes the history of Marks and Spencer. Fill in the blanks using words from exercises 2 and 3. Use the plural form where necessary.

The origins of Marks and Spencer, Britain's best known [1]..........................., go back to 1882 when a Russian refugee, Michael Marks, began selling simple household products from door to door, in villages in North East England. In 1884 he set up a stall in Leeds Kirkgate market and to overcome his language problem, he made a sign displaying his [2].......................... : 'Don't ask the price, it's a penny'. By 1894 Marks had eight stalls and had invited Tom Spencer to join him in what was to become one of the most famous business partnerships in British history.

By the 1920s Marks and Spencer stores were selling some food as well as household products, but the first extensive expansion of the [3].......................... came in the early 1930s when canned goods, cake, fruit and vegetables were introduced. Today Marks and Spencer sells a wide variety of products in over 670 stores worldwide. They have a 16 per cent share of the UK clothing market, a position they maintain by insisting that their [4].......................... manufacture new collections up to one year in advance of the season. The clothes are sold under their own label *St Michael*, which has become a [5].......................... in the British fashion industry.

Marks and Spencer's [6].......................... for the financial year 1990 was £389 million.

DISCUSSION

Read the following excerpts from a Richer Sounds' catalogue. What do you think of the company's approach to customer service? In your country, how important is customer service? Could it be improved?

THE UK'S BUSIEST HI-FI STORES –
...and we still put the customer first!

FREE HI-FI GUIDE
– the jargon explained!

For your convenience and information, we publish a completely **free** concise hi-fi guide which is available at any store or by simply asking for our free guide on **FREEPHONE 0800 591 366 (24hrs).**

Don't be shy!

Unlike most hi-fi stores our aim is definitely **not** to intimidate first time buyers especially if you're more familiar with a 'gramophone' than today's equivalent. If it's your first system tell our sales assistants who will be particularly helpful.

Pets welcome!

You're free to bring along Mutley, Spot, Lucky, Marmalade or Fido to help you make your choice.

About Us...

For your convenience we've printed an information leaflet about our company telling you what we do, who we are and how we do it! Pick up a copy in store or ask for "About Us" on **FREEPHONE 0800 591 366 (24hrs).**

You'll be singing in the rain!

All customers purchasing hi-fi when it's raining, just ask and you'll receive absolutely free a super automatic umbrella.

Thank-you

for your support and for making us the UK's most successful hi-fi retailer. In order to maintain our No.1 position we need to know where we've gone wrong. Suggestions or comments regarding customer service, however small are gratefully received. Every one has Mr. Richer's personal attention and will receive a reply where appropriate. Please, please, please let us know as we really do care!

Write to:
Julian Richer
Richer Sounds
FREEPOST
London SE1 4BR.
(include daytime 'phone number)
No stamp required.

WE'LL BEAT THAT PRICE 'TIL IT HURTS!

We want your business even if it means losing money! If you've seen it cheaper' we'll beat that price by £10 with a smile!

LANGUAGE FOCUS

MAKE AND DO

Look at the following sentences from the text:

*Richer sounds **made profits** of more than £500,000 ....* (line *20*)
*Suppliers are keen to **do business** with this quirky retailer.* (line *73*)

➤➤ *Make* and *do* are very similar in meaning and it is not always easy to know which to use. Turn to page 156 for some guidelines.

Practice

1 *Make* or *do*? Arrange the following words in two columns. Use a dictionary if you are not sure.

a suggestion	a complaint
a decision	the typing
business	a speech
nothing	a job
an exam	your best
research	a sound
a mistake	a trip
damage	a loss

Make	Do
....	....
....	....
....	....
....	....
....	....
....	....
....	....
....	....

2 Complete the following sentences using an appropriate form of *make* or *do* and one of the nouns in exercise 1.

1 Price is not the only thing customers consider when .... a .... about which product to buy.

2 Since the early 1980s, many manufacturers .... into the development of environmentally safe products.

3 Many retailers are breaking the law by .... on Sunday.

4 A .... by a customer about the poor quality of some frozen foods on sale in our stores.

5 We .... a .... last year of nearly £10,000.

3 Choose five other nouns from exercise 1 and write similar sentences.

LOCATING OBJECTS

Do this quick-check exercise as preparation for the listening activity that follows.

Look at this picture of a gift shop and complete the sentences with the words in the boxes.

at the front	in the middle
at the back	on the left
at the top	on the right
at the bottom	

The personal stereos are [1].............................. of a large display cabinet, [2]..............................
of some small radios. The hi-fi systems are [3].............................. of the cabinet and the radio
cassette recorders are [4].............................. . [5].............................. is a smaller display case
containing a selection of jewellery: there are some earrings [6].............................. and some
bracelets [7].............................. .

above	behind
next to	below
between	inside
in front of	

8 The jewellery is .... the perfume counter.

9 The binoculars are on the shelf .... the video cameras.

10 The scarves are .... the perfume counter.

11 There are some video cassettes .... a basket.

12 There is a 'Sale' sign .... the jewellery counter.

13 The watches are .... the earrings and the bracelets.

14 The shop assistant is standing .... the perfume counter.

SKILLS FOCUS

LISTENING

1 You will hear a British supermarket manager talking about the layout and design of her store. Listen and indicate on the floor plan where the following items are located.

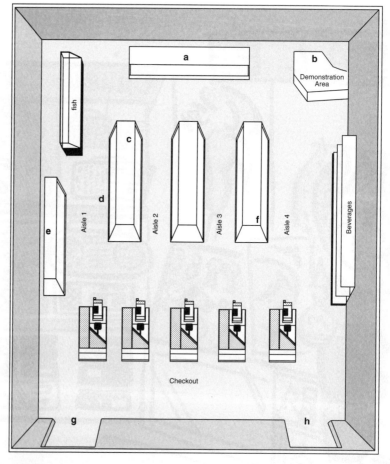

2 Listen again and write down the reasons mentioned for laying out the store in this way.

SPEAKING   **1** With a partner, look at the following list and choose a product which one of you has recently purchased. This person will assume the role of Student A.

- moped, motorcycle, bicycle
- computer, software, calculator
- photographic or video equipment
- watch, jewellery, accessories
- clothing
- sports equipment
- hi-fi or audio equipment
- records, tapes, compact discs

Student A should look at the instructions below and Student B at the instructions on page 149.

Student A
Prepare notes on your reasons for buying the product and for choosing the shop in which you bought it. Did you intend to buy the product before shopping, or did you buy it on impulse? Had you bought this type of product before? Was it your first time in the shop? How would you describe the service, the prices and the overall atmosphere of the shop? Are you satisfied with your purchase?

When you have finished, answer Student B's questions.

2 As a class, determine what made the majority of those playing the part of Student A buy their product. Was it the result of a carefully planned process or a sudden decision to buy? Were most people satisfied with their purchase and the service they received? Were there any serious complaints?

WRITING   Write a short profile of the two people represented in the photos below describing (a) what you imagine their professions to be, and (b) the type of products and services on which they spend their income.

Banking

KEY VOCABULARY

The banking sector in the United Kingdom is made up of a variety of different institutions which are supervised by the country's central bank, **The Bank of England**. This bank not only looks after both the government's finance and monetary policy but it also acts as banker to other banks. However, for the general public and many businesses, banking services are provided by the **Commercial Banks** (also called the **Clearing Banks**) which have offices or **branches** throughout the country. These banks offer a wide range of banking services which include accepting deposits, making loans and managing their customers' accounts. **Merchant Banks**, on the other hand, do not deal with the public in general but specialise in providing services to companies or corporate customers. They are particularly active in arranging mergers and acquisitions and in advising on aspects of corporate finance.

LEAD-IN

1 In pairs make a list of the different services that banks in your country make available to their customers. Put a tick next to the services which you actually use.

Example: *current account* ✓

2 You will hear Peter Milson, a branch manager of the Midland Bank, describing the bank that he manages. As you listen take notes using the headings below to help you:

Location:	....
Number of customers:	....
Opening hours:	....
Services offered:	....
Number of employees:	....
Role in the community:	....

How do the services offered by this bank compare with those available from a bank of a similar size in your country?

MIDLAND

3 The illustration below shows some of the everyday items and documents that are used in banking. Match each of these with the appropriate term from the following list.

1 chequebook

2 bank statement

3 credit card or debit card

4 bill

5 traveller's cheques

6 bank notes

7 coins

8 keyboard

9 screen

10 cash machine

4 Which of the items would you use if you needed to:

1 check how much money you had in your bank account two weeks ago

2 take money with you for a visit to a foreign country

3 see how much you must pay for the electricity you used last month

4 send payment by post

5 take money out of your account on a Sunday

HOBS

HOBS

Pay bills before breakfast . . . invest over lunch . . . and check balances at bedtime. HOBS is the essential banking service for busy people. It allows you to carry out transactions
5 from your home or office when it suits you. You can check the balances of all your accounts with Bank of Scotland whether they are business accounts or personal accounts; view
10 your last 600 transactions on-screen; transfer between your accounts; pay regular bills and even keep a record of them; order a statement or a cheque book and for business users, our special Cash Management Service enables you to see what your cleared balances are, up to 2 days ahead.
15 All these services can be easily accessed using our compact integral keyboard and screen which can be

The Banking service for busy people

purchased for a single payment of only £95, with an option of spreading the cost over ten months. However, the unit will be supplied free of charge to customers who undertake to keep a minimum credit balance of £500 in their Current Account for at least two years. As the unit only takes up approximately the same space as an A4 sheet of paper, it can easily be
30 accommodated on a desk or table. Alternatively, HOBS can be linked to your PC. In addition, no matter where you live in the UK you can access HOBS for the cost of a local telephone call.

Settle bills when it suits you

Regular bills and accounts can be paid by electronic transfer without writing cheques, saving you time and postage. And our Bank charge for an electronic payment is much less than for a cheque.
HOBS even has a memory, which allows you to
40 instruct payment of regular household accounts or invoices up to 30 days in advance, freeing your money to work for you.
You can pay invoices, utility bills and many others. Because the transaction is made on the day you want it,
45 you can keep the funds earning interest until the very last moment.

The special high interest HOBS Investment Account is designed for busy people who want to make the most of their money.

High interest daily

It allows you to organise your finances so that you can earn high interest without locking your money away.
At the touch of a button, you can 55 switch funds from your current account into your HOBS Investment Account. Interest is calculated daily, so you always get the benefit of a healthy balance, even on funds deposited overnight.
All instructions made before 5pm on any business day 60 are carried out that day. After 5pm, they are effective on the next business day.

HOBS opens for business at 7am – so much

Open 18 hours a day

for banking hours! Now you can organise your personal 65 finances before you set off for work and keep tighter control of your business bank accounts from your office at any time throughout the day.

With HOBS, you can bank until 1 o'clock in the morning during the week; and you can bank all day Saturday and Sunday until 11pm. 75

Old-fashioned banking deals with what happened yesterday. HOBS tells you where you stand today and helps you plan ahead.

Look ahead with HOBS

You can also call on Bank of Scotland's expertise for advice on all aspects of finance.
Bank of Scotland offers all the banking services you need as an individual or as a businessman and HOBS is the seven day link to a full clearing bank service, wherever you are in the UK. 85

BANK OF SCOTLAND
A FRIEND FOR LIFE

READING

1 Read the extract from a brochure describing the Bank of Scotland's Home and Office Banking System (HOBS) on the previous page. Then decide if the following statements are true or false.

	T	F

1 HOBS can be used by both business people and private individuals.

2 You can only use HOBS if you have a personal computer.

3 £500 is the minimum required to open a HOBS account.

4 HOBS is only available to residents of Scotland.

5 Making a payment with the HOBS system is more expensive than paying by cheque.

6 HOBS can be programmed to pay your bills automatically.

7 There is more than one type of HOBS account.

8 HOBS is open everyday from 7 a.m. to 1 a.m.

2 Look at the following statements about the HOBS system and put a cross (X) against those which do not appear in the text.

1 If you use HOBS you will be given an identity number and a password.

2 You can make ten monthly payments to cover the cost of buying HOBS.

3 The Bank of Scotland charges customers £10 a month for using HOBS.

4 If you want to take advantage of the Cash Management Service this will cost you extra.

5 You can arrange for The Bank of Scotland to give you a personal demonstration of how HOBS works.

6 The HOBS terminal can fit into a small space.

3 Read through the text again and make a list of the advantages for the customer of using the HOBS system.

DISCUSSION

1 Now that you have considered the benefits that HOBS offers its customers, discuss what, in your opinion, the Bank of Scotland can gain from the introduction of its new system.

2 Are there any similar services to HOBS available in your country? Who provides them and how do they operate?

VOCABULARY

1 Match the words from the text with their corresponding definitions.

1	balance (*line 2*)	**a**	a sum of money exchanged for goods or services
2	transaction (*line 4*)	**b**	to move or change something suddenly
3	purchase (*line 17*)	**c**	specialised knowledge
4	payment (*line 18*)	**d**	the cost of sending letters, parcels etc by mail
5	option (*line 19*)	**e**	amounts of money
6	free of charge (*line 23*)	**f**	a document which lists the goods you have bought and tells you how much you must pay for them
7	postage (*line 37*)	**g**	a choice or alternative
8	invoice (*line 41*)	**h**	to buy
9	funds (*line 45*)	**i**	a movement of money into or out of an account
10	interest (*line 45*)	**j**	to place money in a bank account
11	switch (*line 56*)	**k**	an advantage
12	benefit (*line 58*)	**l**	without cost
13	deposit (*line 59*)	**m**	the amount of money in a bank account at a particular time
14	expertise (*line 81*)	**n**	money paid to someone who invests money

2 Study the information in the bank statement on the opposite page, then complete the passage with the words in the box.

credit	payment	cheque	account
balance	debit	cash	deposit
debit card	transactions		

Jane Sadler opened her [1]............................ with the Medway Bank on 28th January 1993, with a cash [2]............................ of £300. On 15th February she wrote a [3]............................ for £53.25 and this appeared as a [4]............................ on the bank statement on 20th February. On 22nd February she took out £60 in [5]............................ from a cashpoint machine. On the following day the bank debited her account by £33.50 for a [6]............................ she had made using her [7]............................ Her monthly salary was paid directly into her account and this appeared as a [8]............................ for £802.20 on 26thFebruary. There were no further [9]............................ on her account and she finished the month with a [10]............................ of £955.45.

MEDWAY BANK

STATEMENT OF ACCOUNT

CLAPHAM HIGH STREET
LONDON SW4

CURRENT ACCOUNT

MS JANE SADLER
75 EBURY MEWS
LONDON SW5

02–26–56
ACCOUNT NUMBER 54863472
STATEMENT NUMBER 01

STATEMENT DATE 1 MAR 199_

DATE	DETAILS		DEBITS	CREDITS	BALANCE
28 JAN	OPENING DEPOSIT	CSH		300.00	300.00
20 FEB	CHEQUE 000001	CHQ	53.25		246.75
22 FEB	AUTOBANK AB69301 OXFORD ST	CSH	60.00		186.75
23 FEB	WATERSTONE AND CO.	DD	33.50		153.25
26 FEB	BENNET AND SONS	TR		802.20	955.45

ABBREVIATIONS: CHQ – CHEQUE   CSH – CASH   DD – DIRECT DEBIT   TR – TRANSFER

LANGUAGE FOCUS

ALLOW/ENABLE/LET

The verbs *allow* and *enable* can be used to express possibility. Look at the following examples from the text.

*It **allows** you to carry out transactions . . . when it suits you.* (line 4)
*. . . our special Cash Management Service **enables** you to see what your cleared balances are . . . .*(line 13)

The same idea can be expressed using the verb *let*.

*HOBS **lets** users transfer money between accounts at the touch of a button.*

Note that *allow* and *enable* are followed by an object and an infinitive with *to*, but that *let* is followed by an object and an infinitive without *to*.

Practice

Write a sentence about each of the following inventions using the verbs you have just studied.

Example: *A cashpoint card allows you to withdraw money at any time of the day.*

1   A fax machine...

2   A portable computer ....

3   A modem ....

4   A carphone...

5   A credit card ....

FIRST AND SECOND CONDITIONAL

Look at these sentences, then complete the exercise that follows with the words in the box.

A *If you transfer your money to a deposit account,* you'll earn more interest.

B *If I had more money, I'd invest it on the Stock Exchange.*

second conditional	may possibly happen
is unlikely to happen	first conditional

Sentence A is an example of the .... The conditional clause (in bold) refers to a situation that ....

Sentence B is an example of the .... The conditional clause (in bold) refers to a situation that ....

➤➤ For more information on the first and second conditional, turn to page 156.

Practice

1 Complete the following conditional sentences with the verb of your choice. Make sure that you use the correct tense.

1 If I go to Spain next week, I .... to change some money into pesetas.

2 If I lost my credit card, I .... my bank immediately.

3 If I wanted to buy a new car, I .... my bank manager for a loan.

4 If I find any more mistakes on my bank statement, I .... banks.

5 If I earn more money next year, I .... a savings account.

6 If I order a credit card now, ... it before the end of the month?

2 Work in pairs (Student A and Student B). You both have a number of problems, which are listed below. Take it in turns to give each other advice, using *If I were you, I'd . . . .*

Student A's problems

1 You have an important business meeting this afternoon, but you are not feeling well.

2 Your boss entrusted you with a highly confidential report to read over the weekend. You now cannot find it and think you may have left it on the train.

3 You have been sent to a foreign country to negotiate an important new contract for your firm. However, during the negotiations your counterpart makes it clear to you that if your company is to be selected then he will need a personal cash contribution (a bribe) from you.

Student B's problems

1 You lied on your CV about your qualifications in order to get the job you wanted. You have just been offered the job, but your new employer has asked to see your certificates.

2 Two years ago your company signed an agreement to become the exclusive agent for importing kitchen equipment from a Swedish supplier. Recently you have been disappointed to see that another company is now selling the same products and at a lower price.

3 You have just opened your monthly pay packet to find that you have been overpaid by almost £500.

SKILLS FOCUS

SPEAKING

Work in pairs (Student A and Student B). Student A should look at the information below, and Student B at the information on page 150.

Student A

You wish to deposit £30,000 with a bank and have been advised that the Lombard Bank provides very favourable conditions to investors. You have obtained a leaflet about their services, but you require further details before deciding in which account(s) to invest your money. You have therefore arranged to meet a representative of the bank (Student B) who will answer any enquiries that you have. Your saving requirements are as follows:

You wish to set aside a sum of money for your three children, to be divided amongst them on their eighteenth birthdays. Their present ages are 10, 12 and 14.

You would also like to set aside an amount for use in emergencies, for example to carry out any unexpected repairs to your house, to pay medical bills etc.

Total = £30,000

Lombard Bank
Information for savers and investors

Notice Deposit Accounts
A flexible account that offers you easy access to your funds, with deposit periods of 14 days, 3 months and 6 months with no maximum limit to funds deposited.

Fixed Deposit Accounts
The ideal deposit account for those wishing to invest in the longer term with deposit periods ranging from 1 to 5 years. Interest is fixed and guaranteed not to change during the deposit period selected.

Cheque Savings Accounts
A special kind of deposit account which is particularly suitable for those customers who want their savings readily available whilst earning a good rate of interest. A cheque book is supplied and provides the benefits of instant access to your funds.
Whatever your choice you can be assured that a Lombard deposit account will be a secure and confidential home for your money.

Study the leaflet carefully and draw up a list of questions that you will need to ask. The following guidelines show the sort of information you should obtain.

- Minimum/Maximum opening deposits
- Interest rates
- Dates of interest payments
- Restrictions on withdrawing money

Useful language:

Asking for general information

Could you tell me more about …

I'd like some further information on …

Asking for more detailed information

How much interest would I earn if I opened a 3-month notice deposit account?

Would I be able to withdraw funds at short notice from a fixed deposit account?

How often would I be paid interest with a cheque savings account?

When you have finished preparing your questions, you should meet up with Student B. Make notes on the answers you receive and decide how you are going to invest your money.

LISTENING

You will hear Alain Depussé, a financial director for a French company, talking about the relationship between a company and its banks.

1 Listen to the first extract, in which Alain Depussé introduces himself, and answer the following questions.

1 What type of company does he work for?

2 Where is his company based?

3 What experience does he have?

2 In the second extract Mr Depussé talks about the services that a company should expect from a commercial bank. Before you listen, make sure you understand the following terms:

balance sheet: a statement showing the financial position of a company at a certain date

annual report: a document which a company produces every year describing its performance and future objectives

Now listen and complete the table to show a) the type of services which a bank should provide to a company, and b) the type of information which a company should provide to its bank.

Services provided by bank	Information provided by company
• cheap	....
• lowest possible............................	....
• ....answers	....
• reliable	....
• ....commitments	....

What reasons does Alain Depussé give for only providing the bank with a certain amount of information?

3 In the final extract Mr Depussé talks about the relationship between a company and a merchant bank. This is quite different from the relationship which you heard about in extract 2, between a company and a commercial bank.

1 Listen and identify the main difference in terms of the type of information provided by the company. What are the reasons for this difference?

2 Look at the following list of services that a merchant bank may provide. Listen again and decide which of these Mr Depussé actually mentions. (Y = Yes, he mentions them; N = No, he doesn't.)

A merchant bank may:

	Y	N
a provide assistance with raising capital and issuing shares		
b inform companies of potential dangers, including competitors' activities		
c offer standard banking services		
d help to finance international trade and exports		
e provide advice and financial help to companies wishing to form partnerships		

WRITING   Last month you received your bank statement and noticed that your account was overdrawn. After phoning your bank, they informed you that they had mistakenly transferred £500 from your main account into your second account, instead of vice versa. The bank apologised for the error and promised that there would be no overdraft charges. However, you have just received your latest bank statement, on which a £30 overdraft charge appears. You have phoned your bank again to complain and they have advised you to confirm your complaint in writing. Write a short letter to your branch manager in which you state what your complaint is and how you want the bank to correct the mistake.

The address of your bank is:

National Savings Bank
509 Wellington Street
London SW1V 9AW

The Stock Exchange

KEY VOCABULARY

When a company needs to raise money in order to grow, it can choose between two different options. It can issue **shares** (or parts of its capital) which can be bought by the general public. These shares are known as **equities** or **ordinary shares**, and are the most common form of share. When you buy shares in a company, you become a **shareholder** and own a part of (or have a **stake** in) that company. As part owner of a company, you can therefore make or lose money depending on the company's profits. If the company does make profits, it pays a sum of money per share, known as a **dividend**, to its shareholders usually twice a year. Companies can also borrow money from a bank or from the general public by issuing **bonds** which are loans with a fixed amount of interest to be paid each year.

Each year, billions of pounds of shares are bought or sold (or **traded**) on the London Stock Exchange. In addition to the shares mentioned above, **government stocks**, or **gilt-edged securities** are also traded. These are loans issued by the government to help it fund its spending (building roads and hospitals, defence, etc.)

LEAD-IN

Many companies are authorised to use the Stock Exchange to trade their shares. Every day, the press gives prices and other information about the shares of these **listed companies**. In groups, read the following newspaper headlines and decide in each case whether they reflect a good or poor performance of the company's shares on the Stock Exchange.

Example:

General Cinema sees $20 million gain

The shares of this company are doing well since there has been a gain.

1

A. Cohen falls 57% to £555,000

2

XIR share prices sink to lowest level since 1988

3

AMD advances 14%

4

Jones & Shipman: £2.5m in loss as recession bites

5

Scottish and Newcastle rises on all fronts

READING

1 Below you will find answers to five different questions. Read the first three paragraphs of the text on the following page and try to supply the missing questions.

Example: *What is the Stock Exchange?*
It is a place where securities are bought and sold.

1 ....?
They are also called 'gilt-edged securities'.

2 ....?
£570 billion.

3 ....?
Pension schemes, life assurance or subscriptions to a trade union.

4 ....?
TSB, British Gas and Rolls Royce.

5 ....?
27th October 1986.

The Stock Exchange

The Stock Exchange is a market place where securities are bought and sold. These are shares in over 7,000 companies and government stocks which are known as gilt-edged securities. In one year stocks and shares worth over £570 billion change hands.

Most adults in this country save or invest in one form or another and much of these savings will be channelled through the Stock Exchange. This investment might be direct – perhaps buying shares in one of the companies which have recently come onto the market, such as TSB, British Gas, Virgin, Rolls Royce and British Airways. The investment might be indirect – anyone who pays into a pension scheme, has life assurance or subscribes to a trade union is probably investing on the Stock Exchange as this is where a large part of the institutions' funds are invested.

You have probably seen pictures of the Stock Exchange showing a crowded trading floor with throngs of dark suited men milling around hexagonal stands. This indeed was the picture until 27th October, 1986 – the day commonly known as 'Big Bang' which resulted in the greatest changes in the history of the Stock Exchange.

Before Big Bang

Stock Exchange members were either brokers or jobbers. Brokers acted on behalf of their clients to buy and sell shares. Jobbers acted as wholesalers on their own behalf buying from, and selling to, brokers but not to the general public.

An Example

If you had wanted to buy some shares in British Telecom you would have gone to your stockbroker, or your bank who would have instructed their stockbroker to act on your behalf, and given instructions. The stockbroker's office would have telephoned their broker on the floor of the Stock Exchange. He would

then have gone from jobber to jobber asking them to quote a price for British Telecom but without saying whether he wanted to buy or sell. The jobbers would have quoted two prices, say 187–190 (that is the price in pence of each share) the first price being the one at which they were prepared to buy and the second at which they would sell. Your broker would have done the transaction with the jobber who offered the lowest price at which he would sell shares to you. Had you been selling shares your broker would have dealt with the jobber who offered the highest price at which he would buy from you.

The Changes

- Instead of brokers and jobbers, all member firms operate as 'dual capacity' broker/dealers which means that they are free to buy securities from, or sell them to, clients without dealing through a jobber. Some such members – called Market Makers – will undertake to make markets in certain ranges of shares rather as a jobber did in the past.

- Membership of the Stock Exchange, which in the past had only been open to individuals, is now open to corporate members. This has enabled banks, financial institutions, insurance companies and foreign securities firms to become members. Because of their size and capital they are able to compete internationally. This became necessary because as

membership was limited to individuals who, although they grouped themselves into partnerships, were too small to compete with their counterparts abroad, particularly in America and Japan.

- The scale of commission charged for buying and selling shares was scrapped. Since October 27th, 1986 stockbrokers have been able to fix their own charges according to the service they provide.

- To cope with the increased business with which the Stock Exchange has to manage, and to coincide with 'Big Bang', a sophisticated new electronic dealing system has been introduced called SEAQ.

New Technology

SEAQ – Stock Exchange Automated Quotations – shows information on share prices which until 'Big Bang' was only available on the Stock Exchange floor. The information is shown on television screens in brokers' offices anywhere in the UK or overseas giving them all access to the same information simultaneously.

The information is updated continuously as market makers inform the SEAQ central system of trading of what has taken place. The introduction of this sophisticated system has resulted in trading taking place over a television screen rather than on the market floor.

Banking Information Service

2 Read the following statements and decide whether they describe the Stock Exchange as it was before 'Big Bang' (B), or as it is now (N).

	B	N
1 Trading is done by walking around the floor of the Stock Exchange.		
2 Foreign firms operate on the London Stock Exchange.		
3 Stockbrokers fix their own commissions for buying and selling shares.		
4 Jobbers sell shares to, and buy shares from, brokers.		
5 Trading is done through electronic dealing systems.		
6 Information on share prices is available to brokers throughout the world.		

VOCABULARY

1 Choose the word or phrase which best completes each sentence.

1 .... is the general term used for all types of stocks and shares.
    a Gilt-edged   **b** Investment   **c** Securities

2 A .... is an organisation which defends the wages and rights of the workers who belong to it.
    a pension scheme   **b** life assurance   **c** trade union

3 The part of the Stock Exchange where shares are bought and sold is called the ....
    a floor   **b** market place   **c** screen

4 .... advise their clients of what investments to make and act as agents in buying and selling shares.
    a Wholesalers   **b** Counterparts   **c** Brokers

5 To .... a price means to give the price at which one is prepared to buy or sell a share.
    a act   **b** quote   **c** undertake

6 A business deal done between two people is known as a(n) ....
    a instruction   **b** transaction   **c** membership

7 The total wealth of a company in terms of money and property is called ....
    a funds   **b** capital   **c** charges

8 The information contained in the SEAQ system is constantly .... to keep up with changes in the market.
    a automated   **b** updated   **c** traded

2 Complete each sentence with the correct form of the words on the left.

1 to save   He invested most of his .... in the Stock Exchange.

2 to invest   My stockbroker advised me to make several safe ....

3 to compete   .... on the personal computer market has increased considerably over the past few years.

4 partnership   Both .... in the business agree that hard work is the key to their success.

5 to quote   The prices given for buying and selling shares on the Stock Exchange are known as ....

6 member   Trade union .... has declined in the United States.

3 The screen below shows the type of information that is available through SEAQ. Working with a partner, try and match the labels (a-g) to the screen.

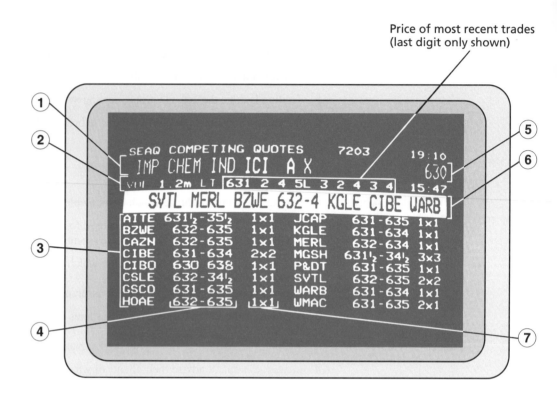

Price of most recent trades (last digit only shown)

a Volume of trading which has taken place so far today

b MARKET MAKERS' quotations for buying/selling shares

c MARKET MAKERS offering best buying/selling prices

d Quantity of shares, in thousands, Market Makers are prepared to buy and sell at the prices quoted

e Name of company/share

f Last night's closing price

g Identification of MARKET MAKERS

Now listen to the cassette and check your answers. A speaker is explaining the SEAQ screen to a group of visitors to the Stock Exchange.

DISCUSSION

Thorntons is a family business which has been making and selling chocolates since 1911. It recently decided that it needed to raise more capital as part of an expansion programme and in order to buy other companies in the UK and abroad. The company therefore 'went public', that is, it issued shares on the stock market. Thorntons set up a special scheme to encourage its employees to acquire shares in the company and it has proved very successful.

In groups, discuss the advantages of acquiring a stake in the company you work for. Make a list and present your findings to the class.

LANGUAGE FOCUS

THIRD CONDITIONAL

Look at the following sentences:

If I had more money, I would invest it on the Stock Exchange.
If I'd had more money, I would have invested it on the Stock Exchange.

What is the difference in meaning between the two sentences? Which one is an example of the third conditional?

➤➤ For more information on the third conditional, turn to page 156.

Practice

Look at the following charts and graphs and complete each sentence using a third conditional structure.

Example: *If I had opened a savings account with £10,000, I would have received 9.35% interest.*

Premium Savings Account

	Gross rate p.a. (%)
£25,000 plus	**9.65**
£10,000 – £24,999	**9.35**
£500 – £9,999	**8.65**

1 If I had worked as a sales assistant at Fashion World Clothing in 1990, ...

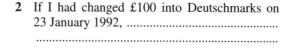

Cashier:	£3.40
Sales Assistant:	£3.60
Book-keeper:	£4.70
Assistant Manager:	£5.10

Hourly wages at Fashion World Clothing (March 1990)

£ buys

Deutschmarks	2.86
Francs	9.76
Lira	2153.50
Pesetas	180.94

2 If I had changed £100 into Deutschmarks on 23 January 1992, ...

3 If I had taken flight LF 903 from Hamburg on 17 October 1992, ...

Flight	From	Comments
AF 231	PARIS	on time
LF 903	HAMBURG	delayed
KLM 090	AMSTERDAM	cancelled
SAS 495	STOCKHOLM	on time

Heathrow Airport flight arrivals (17 October 1992)

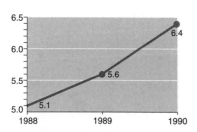

£8,100 £7,500 £6,600 £5,200

1987 1988 1989 1990

Average sales price of a 1986 Renault 25

4 If I'd sold my Renault in 1988, ...

5 ...., I would have paid £245.

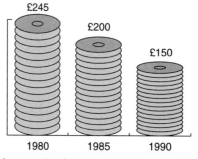

£245 £200 £150

1980 1985 1990

Average price of a compact disc player

6 ...., I would have received a dividend of £5.60.

6.5
6.0
5.5
5.0
5.1 5.6 6.4
1988 1989 1990

Marks and Spencer: dividends per ordinary share (in pence)

SKILLS FOCUS

READING

Many newspapers have a financial section, which includes information about the share prices of listed companies. This information enables you to follow the progress of any shares that you own or that you may be thinking of buying. Look at the explanation of the following listing, then answer the questions opposite.

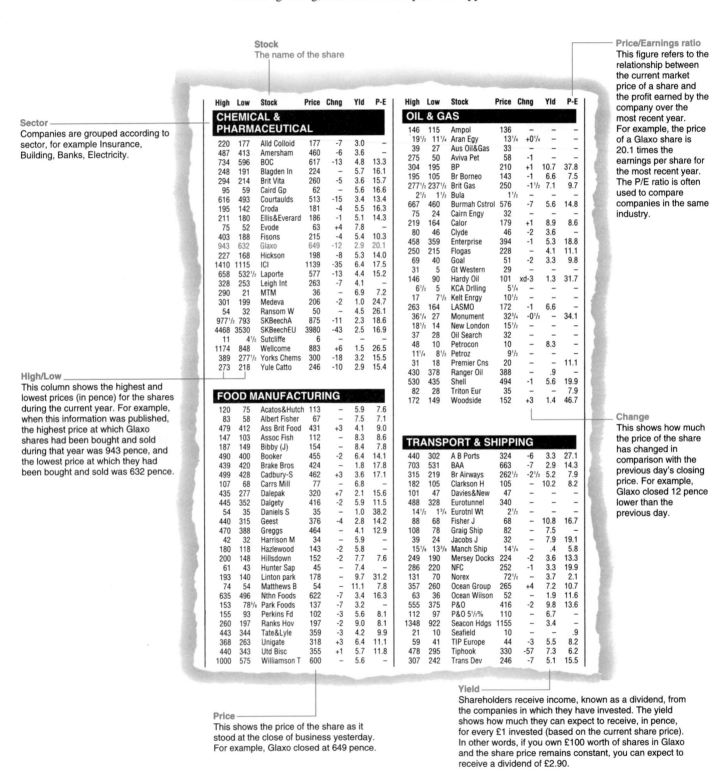

Stock
The name of the share

Sector
Companies are grouped according to sector, for example Insurance, Building, Banks, Electricity.

High/Low
This column shows the highest and lowest prices (in pence) for the shares during the current year. For example, when this information was published, the highest price at which Glaxo shares had been bought and sold during that year was 943 pence, and the lowest price at which they had been bought and sold was 632 pence.

Price
This shows the price of the share as it stood at the close of business yesterday. For example, Glaxo closed at 649 pence.

Price/Earnings ratio
This figure refers to the relationship between the current market price of a share and the profit earned by the company over the most recent year. For example, the price of a Glaxo share is 20.1 times the earnings per share for the most recent year. The P/E ratio is often used to compare companies in the same industry.

Change
This shows how much the price of the share has changed in comparison with the previous day's closing price. For example, Glaxo closed 12 pence lower than the previous day.

Yield
Shareholders receive income, known as a dividend, from the companies in which they have invested. The yield shows how much they can expect to receive, in pence, for every £1 invested (based on the current share price). In other words, if you own £100 worth of shares in Glaxo and the share price remains constant, you can expect to receive a dividend of £2.90.

High	Low	Stock	Price	Chng	Yld	P-E
CHEMICAL & PHARMACEUTICAL						
220	177	Alld Colloid	177	-7	3.0	–
487	413	Amersham	460	-6	3.6	–
734	596	BOC	617	-13	4.8	13.3
248	191	Blagden In	224	–	5.7	16.1
294	214	Brit Vita	260	-5	3.6	15.7
95	59	Caird Gp	62	–	5.6	16.6
616	493	Courtaulds	513	-15	3.4	13.4
195	142	Croda	181	-4	5.5	16.3
211	180	Ellis&Everard	186	-1	5.1	14.3
75	52	Evode	63	+4	7.8	–
403	188	Fisons	215	-4	5.4	10.3
943	632	Glaxo	649	-12	2.9	20.1
227	168	Hickson	198	-8	5.3	14.0
1410	1115	ICI	1139	-35	6.4	17.5
658	532½	Laporte	577	-13	4.4	15.2
328	253	Leigh Int	263	-7	4.1	–
290	21	MTM	36	–	6.9	7.2
301	199	Medeva	206	-2	1.0	24.7
54	32	Ransom W	50	–	4.5	26.1
977½	793	SKBeechA	875	-11	2.3	18.6
4468	3530	SKBeechEU	3980	-43	2.5	16.9
11	4½	Sutcliffe	6	–	–	–
1174	848	Wellcome	883	+6	1.5	26.5
389	277½	Yorks Chems	300	-18	3.2	15.5
273	218	Yule Catto	246	-10	2.9	15.4
FOOD MANUFACTURING						
120	75	Acatos&Hutch	113	–	5.9	7.6
83	58	Albert Fisher	67	–	7.5	7.1
479	412	Ass Brit Food	431	+3	4.1	9.0
147	103	Assoc Fish	112	–	8.3	8.6
187	149	Bibby (J)	154	–	8.4	7.8
490	400	Booker	455	-2	6.4	14.1
439	420	Brake Bros	424	–	1.8	17.8
499	428	Cadbury-S	462	+3	3.6	17.1
107	68	Carrs Mill	77	–	6.8	–
435	277	Dalepak	320	+7	2.1	15.6
445	352	Dalgety	416	-2	5.9	11.5
54	35	Daniels S	35	–	1.0	38.2
440	315	Geest	376	-4	2.8	14.2
470	388	Greggs	464	–	4.1	12.9
42	32	Harrison M	34	–	5.9	–
180	118	Hazlewood	143	-2	5.8	–
200	148	Hillsdown	152	-2	7.7	7.6
61	43	Hunter Sap	45	–	7.4	–
193	140	Linton park	178	–	9.7	31.2
74	54	Matthews B	54	–	11.1	7.8
635	496	Nthn Foods	622	-7	3.4	16.3
153	78⅝	Park Foods	137	-7	3.2	–
155	93	Perkins Fd	102	-3	5.6	8.1
260	197	Ranks Hov	197	-2	9.0	8.1
443	344	Tate&Lyle	359	-3	4.2	9.9
368	263	Unigate	318	+3	6.4	11.1
440	343	Utd Bisc	355	+1	5.7	11.8
1000	575	Williamson T	600	–	5.6	–

High	Low	Stock	Price	Chng	Yld	P-E
OIL & GAS						
146	115	Ampol	136	–	–	–
19½	11¼	Aran Egy	13¼	+0¼	–	–
39	27	Aus Oil&Gas	33	–	–	–
275	50	Aviva Pet	58	-1	–	–
304	195	BP	210	+1	10.7	37.8
195	105	Br Borneo	143	-1	6.6	7.5
277½	237½	Brit Gas	250	-1½	7.1	9.7
2½	1½	Bula	1½	–	–	–
667	460	Burmah Cstrol	576	-7	5.6	14.8
75	24	Cairn Engy	32	–	–	–
219	164	Calor	179	+1	8.9	8.6
80	46	Clyde	46	-2	3.6	–
458	359	Enterprise	394	-1	5.3	18.8
250	215	Flogas	228	–	4.1	11.1
69	40	Goal	51	-2	3.3	9.8
31	5	Gt Western	29	–	–	–
146	90	Hardy Oil	101	xd-3	1.3	31.7
6½	5	KCA Drlling	5¼	–	–	–
17	7½	Kelt Enrgy	10½	–	–	–
263	164	LASMO	172	-1	6.6	–
36¼	27	Monument	32¾	-0½	–	34.1
18½	14	New London	15½	–	–	–
37	28	Oil Search	32	–	–	–
48	10	Petrocon	10	–	8.3	–
11¼	8½	Petroz	9½	–	–	–
31	18	Premier Cns	20	–	–	11.1
430	378	Ranger Oil	388	–	.9	–
530	435	Shell	494	-1	5.6	19.9
82	28	Triton Eur	35	–	–	7.9
172	149	Woodside	152	+3	1.4	46.7
TRANSPORT & SHIPPING						
440	302	A B Ports	324	-6	3.3	27.1
703	531	BAA	663	-7	2.9	14.3
315	219	Br Airways	262½	-2½	5.2	7.9
182	105	Clarkson H	105	–	10.2	8.2
101	47	Davies&New	47	–	–	–
488	328	Eurotunnel	340	–	–	–
14½	1¾	Eurotnl Wt	2½	–	–	–
88	68	Fisher J	68	–	10.8	16.7
108	78	Graig Ship	82	–	7.5	–
39	24	Jacobs J	32	–	7.9	19.1
15⅛	13⅜	Manch Ship	14¼	–	.4	5.8
249	190	Mersey Docks	224	-2	3.6	13.3
286	220	NFC	252	-1	3.3	19.9
131	70	Norex	72½	–	3.7	2.1
357	260	Ocean Group	265	+4	7.2	10.7
63	36	Ocean Wilson	52	–	1.9	11.6
555	375	P&O	416	-2	9.8	13.6
112	97	P&O 5½%	110	–	6.7	–
1348	922	Seacon Hdgs	1155	–	3.4	–
21	10	Seafield	10	–	–	.9
59	41	TIP Europe	44	-3	5.5	8.2
478	295	Tiphook	330	-57	7.3	6.2
307	242	Trans Dev	246	-7	5.1	15.5

1   What was the closing price for each of the following shares?

    a British Petroleum   **c** Cadbury Schweppes
    b British Airways   **d** York Chemicals

2   For each of the four sectors, which shares had the greatest change in price (increase and decrease) compared with the previous day's price?

3   Which of the following oil and gas companies is furthest from its highest price for the year?

    a Great Western   **c** Monument
    b Kelt Energy   **d** Oil Search

4   Which transport and shipping company has a) the highest yield, and b) the lowest yield?

5   What is the price/earnings ratio for each of the following shares?

    a ICI   **c** Ocean Group
    b Geest   **d** Shell

LISTENING 1

You will hear a radio broadcast of a stock market report, given just after the close of business.

1 Before you listen, complete the sentences below with one of the following prepositions and note the different ways of expressing the change in a share's performance.

       down   to   by   from   of   to   at   up

Name of share	Yesterday's closing price	Today's closing price	Change (+/–)
Abbeycrest	92	78	–14
Anglian Water	327	332	+5
Lloyds	400	394	–6
Sun Alliance	300	303	+3
Thames TV	174	180	+6
Ward Holdings	48	48	–
Whitbread	390	387	–3

1   Shares in Anglian Water increased .... 5p.

2   Shares in Abbeycrest fell .... 92p .... 78p.

3   Sun Alliance shares rose 3p .... 303p.

4   Thames TV shares were .... 6p at 180p.

5   There was a drop .... 6p in Lloyds shares.

6   Whitbread shares were .... 3p at 387p.

7   Shares in Ward Holdings stood .... 48p.

2 Now listen and complete the table. Calculate any prices which are not given.

Name of share	Yesterday's closing price	Today's closing price	Change (+/–)
Guinness	542p	....	....
Dixons	....	199p	....
....	373p	....	....
South West Water	....	....	+10p
Sainsbury	359p	....	....
....	....	69p	....
Rolls Royce	....	129p	....
Boots	423p	....	....
British Aerospace	....	....	–3p
National Power	....	144½p	....

SPEAKING

1 Work in pairs or small groups. You have £1000 and are thinking of investing it on the Stock Exchange. Decide which of the shares listed on page 94 you would buy, and calculate how many you could afford. Choose a maximum of four different companies.

Example:

Amersham (Chemical and Pharmaceutical):	50 shares at 460p	=	£230.00
BOC (Chemical and Pharmaceutical):	30 shares at 617p	=	£185.10
Tiphook (Transport and Shipping):	100 shares at 330p	=	£330.00
British Gas (Oil and Gas):	101 shares at 250p	=	£252.50
			£997.60

2 After consideration, you decide not to purchase any shares, but to deposit the £1000 in the bank. However, you are curious to know whether or not you did the right thing. Look at page 152 where you will find the prices for the same shares six months later. Calculate how much money your group would have made or lost if you had bought the shares. Present your findings to the class.

If we had bought ...., we would have | *made* | ....
| *lost* |

WRITING

Read through the financial pages of a newspaper and choose a short article which deals with an announcement or event that will affect or has already affected a company's share prices (for example, redundancies, a natural disaster, a political conflict). Write a brief summary of the article in which you describe how the company's share prices will evolve or have evolved in relation to this event. If no mention is made of this, refer to the relevant listing in the newspaper and check the share price. Has there already been a noticeable increase or decrease?

LISTENING 2

1 Before you listen, look at the following chart.

European stock market turnovers in 1990	(£ million)
Amsterdam	51,969
Athens	2,256
Brussels	9,120
Copenhagen	172,093
Frankfurt	413,178
London	833,319
Madrid	22,492
Milan	45,109
Paris	374,479
Stockholm	8,661

Which European stock exchange has the highest turnover? Can you think of a reason why?

You will hear Stuart Valentine of the London Stock Exchange explaining some of the main differences between various European stock exchanges. Listen and complete the chart.

Stock Exchange	Characteristics
London	
Frankfurt	
Paris	
Stockholm	

2 In the second extract, Stuart Valentine explains how the British public's attitude towards stock ownership and the Stock Market has changed. Listen and label the following figures to show what each one represents.

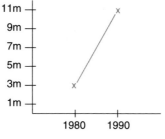

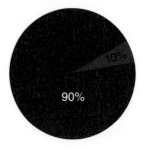

Figure 1:...
....

Figure 2:...
....

Listen again and make a list of the three ways in which people participate in the UK Stock Market.

1 ....
....

2 ....
....

3 ....
....

Corporate Alliances and Acquisitions

KEY VOCABULARY

As business and the world economy become increasingly competitive, more and more companies are having to strengthen their operations to remain profitable. Companies can go about this in a number of ways, including the following:

Joint venture: This is when two or more companies agree to collaborate and jointly invest in a separate business or project. This type of deal allows the partners to combine their strengths in one specific area.

Merger: This is when two companies, often in the same industry, come together to form one company. Companies merge for many reasons, for example, to increase market share and cut costs in certain areas, such as research and development.

Acquisition or **takeover:** This is when one company accumulates enough of another company's shares to take over control and ownership.

LEAD-IN

In pairs, read the following extracts from the financial press. In each case, decide whether they refer to (a) a joint venture, (b) a merger or (c) an acquisition.

1 The biggest deal of the year was carried off by Philip Morris of the US, which bought the Swiss chocolate and coffee group Jacobs Suchard for $2.2 billion.

2 Asea AB of Sweden and Brown Boveri and Company of Switzerland, together have formed the world's largest electrical engineering group with combined sales of $18.6 billion.

3 Two American car makers, General Motors and Chrysler, are combining two of their transmission plants in a new company called 'New Venture Year'.

4 AEG and Deutsche Aerospace, two Daimler Benz subsidiaries, have formed a new group based in Stuttgart. The new project will employ 20,000 workers.

5 The National Australia Bank announced in January its purchase of Yorkshire Bank UK for $1.9 billion.

READING The text below gives details of an alliance that was formed between the two car manufacturers Renault and Volvo at the beginning of the 1990s.

1 Read the text and answer the following questions.

1 What do you understand by the term 'economies of scale'?

2 According to the text, what economies of scale are Volvo and Renault seeking through their alliance?

3 What other economies of scale can large businesses benefit from?

Volvo's Pehr Gyllenhammar and Renault's Raymond Levy announce the deal

Getting Together

Two European automakers strike a powerful alliance

For months, the two companies had been negotiating over a possible corporate partnership. In December the talks broke down, and both firms were said to be
5 looking for alliances elsewhere. Then last week Sweden's Volvo and France's Renault announced that they had reached agreement on a partial melding of their car and truck operations. While the deal
10 falls short of a full merger, it nonetheless creates an automotive powerhouse that will be better able to withstand the pressures of an increasingly competitive European market.
15   Under the terms of the $4.1 billion agreement announced in Amsterdam, Volvo and Renault will swap 45% of the shares in their truck and bus operations and up to 25% of the stock in their car
20 divisions. In addition, Renault, a state-owned company, will acquire 10% of AB

Volvo, the Swedish manufacturer's parent corporation. The companies will enter into an 'extensive co-operation
25 agreement,' under which they will co-ordinate product development, research and component purchases. Describing the deal as 'an alliance, not a merger or an acquisition,' Volvo Chairman Pehr
30 Gyllenhammar said it would give the two companies the 'size, breadth and depth well above the critical mass necessary to survive in this fiercely competitive industry.'
35   The two companies already have a history of co-operation: many of their automobiles, in fact, share the same engines. Renault produces 1.9 million cars a year, while Volvo turns out slightly
40 more than 400,000. Together they will control 20% of the European car market. They will also produce 140,000 trucks,

more than the current European market leader, Daimler-Benz of West Germany.
45 Renault, analysts say, will benefit from Volvo's upscale image and pan-European marketing network, while Volvo will gain a foothold in the post-1992 European Community, of which Sweden is not a
50 member. 'The stock swap makes sense for both sides,' says Paul Capella of the Automotive Group for DRI Europe, a research unit based in London. 'The two companies make a good fit.'
55   While both firms are profitable – Renault earned $1.4 billion in 1988, Volvo about the same – they are also seen as vulnerable to competitive pressures. Renault ranks last in market share among
60 Europe's big-volume automakers and is saddled with huge debts left over from a money-losing period in the early 1980s. Volvo, which saw its profits plunge 14% during the first nine months of 1989, is
65 considered too small to compete effectively in post-1992 Europe.
  The same competitive pressures have resulted in two other marriages of convenience between European
70 automakers in the past four months. In November, Ford Motor Co. announced that it would acquire Britain's Jaguar PLC for $2.5 billion. And in January General Motors bought 50% of the car
75 division of Volvo's Swedish sister Saab-Scania. 'The basic force behind auto mergers in Europe is the single European market,' says Krishan Bhaskar, director of the Motor Industry Research Unit, an
80 independent study group in Britain. 'Companies need more capital and economies of scale to function effectively across more markets.'

– By Michael S. Serrill. Reported by Christopher Redman/Paris and Adam Zagorin/Brussels

Time

2 Indicate whether the following information refers to Renault only, to Volvo only or to both companies.

Example: Produces more than 400,000 cars a year. ....*Volvo*...................

1 Has the lowest market share of the big European car makers. ....

2 Manufactures nearly 2,000,000 cars a year. ....

3 Lost money at the start of the 1980s. ....

4 Will produce more trucks than Daimler-Benz. ....

5 Will benefit from a marketing system which covers all of Europe. ....

6 Made more than $1 billion in 1988. ....

7 Will secure a position in the post-1992 European market. ....

VOCABULARY

1 Complete the following passage with these words from the text.

talks (*line 3*)   foothold (*line 48*)
competitive (*line 13*)   capital (*line 81*)
terms (*line 15*)   economies of scale (*line 82*)
network (*line 47*)   effectively (*line 82*)

Some companies form alliances because they need to combine their technological resources and ¹........................... in order to be more ²........................... in the global market place. Working together greatly reduces production costs thanks to the ³........................... which can only be achieved by very large operations. A company which wants to establish a ⁴........................... in a new market can speed up the process by forming a joint venture with a firm that already has the technology or marketing ⁵........................... that it needs. However, business leaders should make sure during the initial ⁶........................... that the cultures, interests and objectives of the two partners are compatible. Only if both firms fully agree on the ⁷........................... of the contract, will the joint venture's managers have the flexibility and freedom they need to operate ⁸........................... .

2 Look at the following words from the text and complete the table. You may need a dictionary to help you.

Verb	Noun	Adjective
produce	product produce production producer	productive
survive	....	—
....	....	competitive
....	profit	....
....	co-operation	....
....	acquisition	—
negotiate	....	....

DISCUSSION   Study the advertisement below. Why is Motokov advertising? How could they help a company wishing to invest in Eastern Europe?

WE'VE
GROWN

UP

It took a long time, but now the free market has arrived in Central and Eastern Europe. And now, in post-Revolutionary Czechoslovakia, Motokov a.s. is more active than ever in the most competitive Western markets. This year, we expect to double our automotive exports.

Motokov is cooperating with some of the West's largest companies, importing and distributing their products in our markets. We import high technology and raw materials. We arrange joint ventures. We negotiate barter and countertrade. And we provide financial services.

Motokov is Czechoslovakia's largest trading company, with a turnover of about $2 billion a year – and we're one of the largest companies in all of Eastern Europe. We operate 20 subsidiaries in 16 countries on five continents. With business connections in 110 countries, the Motokov family of 1,300 employees has solid experience in virtually every international market.

Traditionally, our main export product lines have been automobiles, trucks, tractors, agricultural machinery and tyres. Our Skoda, Tatra, Zetor and Barum brand names are well-known. But now we're seeking to broaden our horizons with new ventures, bringing our 40 years' experience to new markets.

In Eastern Europe, no one else is big enough, or skilled enough, to fill our shoes.

Tel.: 42.2.414 1111, Telex: 121 882, Fax: 42.2.434 616, Na strži 63, 140 62 Prague, CZECHOSLOVAKIA   **MOTOKOV a.s.**

LANGUAGE FOCUS

REPORTED SPEECH

Look at the following sentence from the text.

Last week Sweden's Volvo and France's Renault announced that they had reached agreement . . . (line 5)

What were the actual words used when this announcement was made? Complete the sentence:

'We .... agreement,' announced Volvo and Renault.

What are the main rules when changing direct speech to reported speech? Think about tenses, pronouns, punctuation and word order.

Practice

1 Notice how the tenses change in the following examples, and complete the table.

Direct speech	Reported speech	Examples	
Present simple	Past simple	1 'Where do you work?'	→ He asked me where I worked.
Present continuous		2 'We're expanding rapidly.'	→ She said that they were expanding rapidly.
	Past perfect	3 'Prices went up in 1992.'	→ He said that prices had gone up in 1992.
Present perfect		4 'Have you finished the report?'	→ She asked if I had finished the report.
	would	5 'I'll probably be late.'	→ She said that she would probably be late.
can		6 'I can't afford it.'	→ He said that he couldn't afford it.

➤➤ For more information on reported speech, turn to page 157.

2 Sarah Hart, Export Manager of a UK manufacturing company, has just returned from Hungary, where she was investigating the possibility of setting up a joint venture. At a meeting to discuss her findings, she made the following comments. Put these into reported speech, using an appropriate verb from the list. Use each verb once only.

add
~~announce~~
confirm
explain
stress

point out
predict
promise
warn

Example:
'I would like to start by saying that I have just completed a detailed study of the Hungarian market.'
She announced that she had just completed a detailed study of the Hungarian market.

1 'It is extremely important – I repeat, extremely important – that the company should negotiate a joint venture with a local manufacturer as soon as possible.'

2 'One thing you may not know is that joint ventures don't require licences in Hungary, only simple registration.'

3 'Another interesting point is that investors enjoy a five-year tax holiday and can import duty-free.'

4 'Of course the conditions for doing business will not be ideal, because of the poor quality of the Hungarian telephone system, for example.'

5 'However, I am certain that this will improve in the next few years.'

6 'It is true that wages are very low in Hungary.'

7 'I guarantee that we will keep labour costs to a minimum.'

8 'Lastly, I would like to draw your attention to the fact that the domestic market will soon be saturated.'

SKILLS FOCUS

LISTENING 1   You will hear a dialogue between a car dealer and a customer requesting technical
information about the BMW 850i. Before you listen, try and complete the conversation
using the following table of specifications.

Model	BMW 850i
Price	£61,950
Type of engine	V12
Engine capacity	4,998 cc
Power	300 b.h.p.
Weight	1,900 kg
Maximum speed	248 k.p.h.
Acceleration from 0-100 k.p.h.	7 secs.

Petrol consumption (per 100 km)
   Town driving
   At 90 k.p.h.
	
	19.8 l.
	8.8 l.

Seating capacity	4

Customer: Hello. I was wondering if you could tell me the name of this model?

Dealer: Yes, of course. It's the 850i, BMW's top of the range luxury coupé.

Customer: ....?

Dealer: It has a 300-horsepower V12 engine of about 5,000 cubic centimetres.

Customer: ....?

Dealer: The maximum speed is 248 kilometres per hour and the car can accelerate
from 0 to 100 kilometres in 7 seconds.

Customer: And what is the seating capacity?

Dealer: As you can see, ...

Customer: Could you tell me how much petrol it uses?

Dealer: That depends on where you're driving. ....
19.8 litres per 100 kilometres in town driving and 8.8 litres per
100 kilometres when driving at 90 kilometres per hour on the open road.

Customer: And one last question: how much does it sell for?

Dealer: The BMW 850i ....

Now listen and write down the words which are actually used.

SPEAKING   Divide into groups of three. Student A should look at the table on page 104, Student B at
the table on page 147, and Student C at the table on page 151. You should then ask and
answer questions like those in the dialogue you have just heard in order to complete your
table with details of all three cars.

SPECIFICATIONS	CAR A	CAR B	CAR C
Model	Fiat Croma 2.0 turbo		
Price	£19,249		
Type of engine	4 cylinder		
Engine capacity	1,995 cc		
Power	158 b.h.p.		
Weight	1,177 kg.		
Maximum speed	212 k.p.h.		
Acceleration from 0-100 k.p.h.	7.7 secs		

Petrol consumption (per 100 km)
    Town driving
    At 90 k.p.h.
	6.0 l.
	3.9 l.		

Seating capacity	4		
Additional information	Electric windows, sunroof, electrically adjusted and heated front seats		

WRITING

You work in the sales and marketing department of a medium-sized electronics company. Your boss has asked you to investigate the possibility of replacing the cars presently used by the four members of the department. The company, which is located outside Brussels, manufactures and distributes machines and equipment for microchip assembly and employs 60 people. You and the other members of the department spend a good deal of time visiting clients in other European countries and attending trade fairs and exhibitions.

With your group, decide which of the three models above would best suit the needs of the department. Then write a brief memo to your boss stating your recommendation and giving reasons for your choice. (Look back at the section on writing a memo on page 58.)

LISTENING 2   **1** You will hear Margareta Galfard, Director of Information and Public Affairs for Volvo, France. For each of the headings (1–7), decide which of the three alternatives (a, b or c) best corresponds to her description of Volvo.

1	Type of company	a	national	b	international	c	multinational
2	Sectors	a	transport aerospace health & food marine	b	transport telecommunications marine aerospace	c	transport industrial products information technology aerospace
3	No. of markets	a	113	b	130	c	1,300
4	No. of employees	a	70,000	b	770,000	c	77,000
5	Stake in Procordia	a	50%	b	approx. 50%	c	60%
6	Market position with Renault	a	the largest automotive company in the world	b	the largest automotive company in Europe	c	the 4th largest truck company in the world
7	Largest market	a	Europe	b	USA	c	Asia

2 In this extract, Ms Galfard talks about some of the advantages of the Renault-Volvo alliance. Listen and take notes under the following headings:

■ Research and Development

■ Quality

■ Components

The Small Business

KEY VOCABULARY

Many of the larger businesses in the UK are **public limited companies** which means that the public is able to buy and sell their shares on the Stock Exchange. Such companies have the letters *plc* after their name, and examples include Marks and Spencer, Guinness and the National Westminster Bank. However, since the minimum share capital for a public limited company is £50,000, this makes it an unsuitable choice for small businesses, which are more likely to take one of the following forms:

Sole Trader or **Sole Proprietor**
This is the simplest way of starting a business. You are self-employed and entirely responsible for all aspects of running your own business. This is especially suitable for small retail businesses.

Partnership
When two or more people want to start a business together they can set up a partnership and agree on how the business will be operated. All partners are responsible for the debts of the partnership and profits and losses are shared between them.

Private Limited Company
A company can be formed with a minimum of two people becoming its shareholders. In order to establish such a company, specific administrative procedures must be followed. For example, the shareholders must appoint a director and a company secretary. If the company goes out of business the responsibility of each shareholder is limited to the amount of money that they have contributed. A private limited company has the letters *Ltd.* (Limited) after its name.

LEAD-IN

1 Look at the following business cards. What type of business does each one correspond to: public limited company, sole trader, partnership or private limited company?

2 Work in pairs. Which of the following advantages and disadvantages would you associate with (a) a sole trader, (b) a partnership, and (c) a private limited company?

Advantages

1   You have total control of your business. ....

2   This is a good way of sharing the pressure and work involved in starting a business. ....

3   The financial risks that you are taking are restricted. ....

4   You can increase your capital by selling shares. ....

Disadvantages

1   There is a danger that conflicts of personality could ruin your business. ....

2   It may be difficult to expand. ....

3   You may have to sell your possessions if the company goes into debt. ....

4   It is complicated and expensive to set up. ....

3 Starting a business always involves a certain amount of planning. Working with a partner, prepare a short checklist of the questions that you would need to ask yourselves before opening a business.

Example:
How much money will I need?

LISTENING

The text which you are about to read describes how Ben Fox, a young British businessman, set up his own company. Before you read, listen to Ben Fox talking about himself and his company, and complete the information below.

1   Age: ....

2   Name of company: ....

3   Nature of business: ....

4   Date of opening: ....

5   Previous employer: ....

6   Reasons for opening the company: ....

....

....

Deliver us from debt

'I THOUGHT it would be easier than running a restaurant. But it's not.' Ben Fox has been learning the hard way since setting up in London last year what he claims is Britain's first hot pasta home delivery service.

A £75,000 bank loan has already been gobbled up. Too much money was consumed on pasta making and cooking machinery. Too much money was ladled into artwork and graphic design. Fox was a little too extravagant with himself, buying a jeep in his own company's livery.

'We could have got the venture going for much less money and still got the same level of business.' he says. 'We certainly have made some mistakes.'

Fasta Pasta, operating from take-away style premises in Fulham, will probably be saved only if discussions between 27-year-old Fox and a couple of potential partners bear fruit. That would mean an injection of new capital and the spreading of overheads by opening at least two further outlets.

When he was made redundant in 1989 from Pizza Piazza, the fast food chain where he was development manager, Fox decided to set up his own fast food business. Pasta was chosen because there are few, if any, home delivery services of linguine, spaghetti, rigatoni and the other variations of the Italians' favourite dish. It is also an increasingly popular food.

'There are now more people in the UK eating pasta but we eat only about seven pounds per person per year compared with ten pounds in the United States and 57 pounds in Italy.'

The concept was to make up pasta dishes with their sauces and deliver them hot by bicycle. Most of the banks Fox approached turned their noses up at the idea. Eventually, his local branch of National Westminster agreed a £72,000 loan of which all but £20,000 is guaranteed under the government's loan guarantee scheme. Fox put in just £3,000 of his own money.

Setting up a business, if you are not careful, can suck up money faster than it can be counted. The property in

Nicholas Garnett meets a young entrepreneur who got on his bike

Spaghetti wheels: Ben Fox of Fasta Pasta

Fulham costs £13,500 a year rent on a 20-year lease with rent reviews every four years. Refurbishing it cost another £8,000 to £10,000. Fox went to Italy and bought pasta and sauce making equipment, mainly from one manufacturer, Prestigiosa, at a total cost of close on £20,000. Five new mountain bikes cost £300 each – though two have since been stolen – and fancy menus and uniforms £4,000.

Fox installed a fax machine and bought books of pre-printed sheets of his own design on which companies could fax lunchtime orders.

'With hindsight, we made a number of mistakes. We ordered too much pasta equipment. I could have done without the jeep. I could have cycled to work or used the Tube. The fax system is not used as avidly as I would have hoped. Unless you are in the centre of the city, I don't think it pays for itself.'

Nevertheless, Fox says he has 'absolutely no doubts' that with further investment a pasta delivery service such as Fasta Pasta can be successful. He

says the business will have a turnover in the first twelve months of about £100,000. About 30 per cent of the company's business is done at lunchtime and overall about a third is for business rather than domestic consumption. All but 5 per cent of the business is delivery, with a small trade in take-outs.

Fasta Pasta's dishes of freshly made-up semolina flour, water, eggs and salt and with sauces ranging from prawns and vodka to good old bolognese vary from £3 to £7. It offers a dozen different types of pasta and a similar number of sauces to more than 500 customers a week. The dishes are delivered to homes and offices, including Virgin and PolyGram, within a 25 minute ride by cycle which carry panniers heat-insulated with radiator lining. Two full time staff are employed with several other people called in when necessary to cope with deliveries. The principal method of promoting the business has been mail drops which Fox says need to be repeated three or four times a year at a cost each time of about £300.

Fasta Pasta, though, is struggling to make any sort of profit. That is in spite of a one year holiday on interest repayments on the business loan. Fox hopes that at least two investors will be putting in between £75,000 and £100,000 and taking a 40 per cent share in the company.

'The intention is to open two further outlets. We would be able to set those up for about £25,000 less than we did with this place in Fulham.' Fulham would then act partly as a centralised kitchen, doing some of the food preparation for the other two outlets.

Fox says that he wants to promote a mix of good value and decent service with healthy eating, stressing that pasta averages 33 calories per ounce (though that is without the sauce).

'We kind of want to make it The Body Shop of fast food.'

The body of the business at the moment, however, is not so healthy and survival without extra finance is going to prove very awkward.

Financial Times

READING **1** According to the article, which of the following statements best summarises Fasta Pasta's present situation:

1 Fasta Pasta has been extremely successful and is about to expand by opening two new outlets.

2 Fasta Pasta is going through a difficult time but hopes that with more money it will survive.

3 Fasta Pasta is losing a lot of money and will probably have to close down.

2 Before a bank will lend money to a small business, it needs certain information about the person who is going to manage it and about the products or services it is planning to sell. Below are some of the questions which a bank may ask. Using information from the article imagine that you are Ben Fox answering these questions at the time that he was thinking of starting his business.

1 What is your product or service?

2 Is there sufficient market demand?

3 What competitive advantages does your business have?

4 Do you have any relevant experience?

5 What type of finance are you looking for?

6 How will you use the money to develop your business?

7 Will you need to invest more money at a later date? How will you obtain this?

8 How will you promote your product or service?

VOCABULARY **1** Match the words from the text with their corresponding definitions.

1	entrepreneur (*subtitle*)	**a**	a request from a customer for a product or service
2	set up (*line 4*)	**b**	to give a new look to something
3	loan (*line 7*)	**c**	the buildings or land owned by an individual or organisation
4	premises (*line 20*)	**d**	the local office of a larger organisation
5	capital (*line 24*)	**e**	an agreement which lets someone use a building or land for a specific period of time
6	branch (*line 46*)	**f**	the buildings where a company is located
7	property (*line 54*)	**g**	a person who starts his or her own business
8	rent (*line 55*)	**h**	the amount of money paid to the owner of a building or land in exchange for its use
9	lease (*line 56*)	**i**	a charge paid to a person who has lent you money
10	refurbish (*line 57*)	**j**	an amount of money borrowed by an individual or company
11	order (*line 69*)	**k**	the money required to start or expand a business
12	interest (*line 112*)	**l**	to make the necessary arrangements for opening a business

2 Richard Green, the owner of a small business, describes how he got started. Complete the sentences using words from the previous exercise. Change the form of the words where necessary.

'At the beginning we calculated that we would need to invest £25,000 to
¹............................ the business. We were able to raise part of this
²............................ by selling a house that we owned. We then negotiated with the
local ³............................ of the bank and they agreed to give us a ⁴............................
of £3,000.

We moved to our current ⁵............................ near Carlisle in North East England in
1989. We did this mainly because the ⁶............................ of £45 a week was so
much cheaper than in the South. Since the building was completely new we didn't
need to spend money on ⁷............................ it. At the moment we have a five-year
⁸............................ which we are hoping to renew.'

DISCUSSION

Working with your partner read the following quotes which describe some of the sacrifices made by people who have started their own businesses. Decide which of these you would be prepared to accept and which you would not.

"I had to sell my house in order to get enough money to start the business. So that meant spending the next three years living in a caravan."

"When I started, my three kids were in school and I had to mortgage our home and put every cent that I had into the business. Then I had to ask friends to put their money in as well."

"At the beginning it was eighteen hours of work a day, seven days a week. It was a total commitment of not just myself but of the whole family."

"I'm earning less than half of my previous salary after 18 months in business."

LANGUAGE FOCUS

**COULD HAVE +
PAST PARTICIPLE**

Look at the following sentences from the text:

*I **could have done** without the jeep.*
*I **could have cycled** to work or used the Tube.*

In both these examples the speaker is expressing an opinion about an action that occurred in the past and saying that there were alternative courses of action available at that time but which were not adopted.

Action: *She came at 10 o'clock.*
Alternative: *She **could have come** earlier.*

Practice

Read the following text and make a list of the decisions that are mentioned. Then, using *could have*, suggest what alternatives were available in each case.

> Richard Simpson used to be a successful financier with the Morgan Grenfell bank in the City of London. However, in early 1991, at the age of 32, he decided to leave his job and buy his own business. The company that he chose to buy was 'Price's Patent Candle Company', an old-fashioned candle manufacturer located in south London, which belonged to Shell. Once he had bought it, Simpson's lifestyle suddenly changed: he took a salary cut of 40%, said goodbye to the company car and moved from his comfortable office into a prefabricated one in the car park. He then decided to bring his father into the business to help him and together they made the decision not to sell Price's subsidiaries. As Simpson says, 'I've got a commitment to the staff and the business.'

Decision	**Alternative**
Richard Simpson left his job.	*He could have continued working for*
	Morgan Grenfell.

SHOULD HAVE + PAST PARTICIPLE

The construction *should have* + past participle is used in two principal ways:

a In the negative to show that, in the speaker's opinion, a particular past action was a mistake or was regrettable.

*He **shouldn't have taken** so long to finish his report.*

b In the affirmative to indicate that there was a better alternative to what was done.

*They **should have reduced** their prices sooner.*

Practice

Work in pairs. The following examples illustrate different mistakes that have been made in business. In each case identify the mistake and then discuss what should have happened.

Example:
After a famous European pen manufacturer had redesigned one of its luxury pens, some customers found that they leaked.

They shouldn't have changed the design. They should have tested the new design more carefully.

1 A company selling fridges in Saudi Arabia included in its brochure a picture of one of its models with the door open and with a smoked ham lying inside.

2 An American car manufacturer launched a new car on the Spanish market under the name 'Nova'.

3 A British food retailer received complaints from its customers in France who had bought its bacon thinking it was country ham.

4 A food company was unsuccessful when trying to market a cake mix to Japanese housewives, by suggesting that it could be cooked in their electric rice cookers.

5 An international bank sent a young woman executive to run its Japanese operation.

6 An American tobacco company had problems when it targeted only black consumers for a new brand of cigarettes.

SKILLS FOCUS

LISTENING

1 You will hear Ben Fox describing how he got the original idea for opening Fasta Pasta. Listen and answer the following questions.

1　What was Ben Fox's job when he worked for the pizza restaurant company?

2　What kind of hours was he working at that time?

3　What observation did he make about the home delivery market?

4　Where did he first see a takeaway pasta operation?

5　Why does Ben Fox call pasta 'the ultimate fast food'?

2 Listen to Ben Fox's description of the customers of Fasta Pasta.

1　What are the differences between the customers he serves (a) at lunchtime and (b) in the evenings?

2　How does he describe the average customer?

3 In this extract, Ben Fox answers the question 'What advice would you give to young people thinking of setting up their own business?' Listen and complete the following pieces of advice with the verbs which he uses.

1　.................................... whatever you want to do carefully

2　.................................... to friends and relatives and people you know about what you want to do

3　.................................... in what you're doing

4　.................................... to people and .... from others

5　.................................... the right sort of background

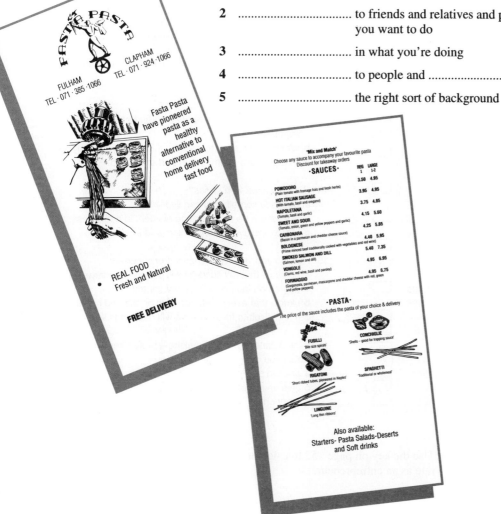

SPEAKING   Have you got what it takes to run your own business? Do the questionnaire and discuss your answers with a partner.

HOW DO YOU RATE AS AN ENTREPRENEUR?

For each of the following questions, tick the answer which comes closest to what you feel about yourself.

1 Are you a self-starter?
a I only make an effort when I want to.
b If someone explains what to do, then I can continue from there.
c I make my own decisions. I don't need anyone to tell me what to do.

2 How do you get on with other people?
a I get on with almost everybody.
b I have my own friends and I don't really need anyone else.
c I don't really feel at home with other people.

3 Can you lead and motivate others?
a Once something is moving I'll join in.
b I'm good at giving orders when I know what to do.
c I can persuade most people to follow me when I start something.

4 Can you take responsibility?
a I like to take charge and to obtain results.
b I'll take charge if I have to but I prefer someone else to be responsible.
c Someone always wants to be the leader and I'm happy to let them do the job.

5 Are you a good organiser?
a I tend to get confused when unexpected problems arise.
b I like to plan exactly what I'm going to do.
c I just let things happen.

6 How good a worker are you?
a I'm willing to work hard for something I really want.
b I find my home environment more stimulating than work.
c Regular work suits me but I don't like it to interfere with my private life.

7 Can you make decisions?
a I am quite happy to execute other people's decisions.
b I often make very quick decisions which usually work but sometimes don't.
c Before making a decision I need time to think it over.

8 Do you enjoy taking risks?
a I always evaluate the exact dangers of any situation.
b I like the excitement of taking big risks.
c For me safety is the most important thing.

9 Can you stay the course?
a The biggest challenge for me is getting a project started.
b If I decide to do something, nothing will stop me.
c If something doesn't go right first time I tend to lose interest.

10 Are you motivated by money?
a For me, job satisfaction cannot be measured in money terms.
b Although money is important to me, I value other things just as much.
c Making money is my main motivation.

11 How do you react to criticism?
a I dislike any form of criticism.
b If people criticize me I always listen and may or may not reject what they have to say.
c When people criticize me there is usually some truth in what they say.

12 Can people believe what you say?
a I try to be honest, but it is sometimes too difficult or too complicated to explain things to other people.
b I don't say things I don't mean.
c When I think I'm right, I don't care what anyone else thinks.

13 Do you delegate?
a I prefer to delegate what I consider to be the least important tasks.
b When I have a job to do I like to do everything myself.
c Delegating is an important part of any job.

14 Can you cope with stress?
a Stress is something I can live with.
b Stress can be a stimulating element in a business.
c I try to avoid situations which lead to stress.

15 How do you view your chances of success?
a I believe that my success will depend to a large degree on factors outside my control.
b I know that everything depends on me and my abilities.
c It is difficult to foresee what will happen in the future.

16 If the business was not making a profit after five years, what would you do?
a give up easily
b give up reluctantly
c carry on

Scoring: Use the key on page 152 to calculate your total score. Then check opposite to see how you rate as an entrepreneur.

44 or above
You definitely have the necessary qualities to become the director of a successful business. You have a strong sense of leadership, you can both organise and motivate and you know exactly where you and your team are going.

between 44 and 22
You may need to think more carefully before setting up your own business. Although you do have some of the essential skills for running a business, you will probably not be able to deal with the pressures and strain that are a part of the job. You should perhaps consider taking some professional training or finding an associate who can compensate for some of your weaknesses.

below 22
Managing your own business is not for you. You are better suited to an environment where you are not responsible for making decisions and taking risks. To operate successfully you need to follow well defined instructions and you prefer work that is both regular and predictable.

WRITING

Many banks offer a specialised service to people wishing to set up their own business. This may include advice on various aspects of starting and running a business, as well as financial assistance in the form of a loan.

Work in pairs/small groups. You have decided to set up your own business together and have approached the bank for advice. They have asked you to prepare a business plan giving information about your proposed business. The list below shows some of the many details you will be required to give. With your partner(s), agree what type of business you are going to set up, then discuss each of the points listed in the business plan. When you have finalised all the details of your business, prepare a written plan to give to the bank.

BUSINESS PLAN FORM

1 DETAILS OF THE BUSINESS
Name of business
Type of business
Format (limited company, partnership etc.)

2 PERSONAL DETAILS
Relevant work experience

3 PERSONNEL
Number of people/job function

4 PRODUCT/SERVICE
Description

5 MARKET
Describe your market
Who are your customers?
Is your market growing, static or in decline?
Who are the main competitors?
What are the advantages of your product or service over the competition?

6 MARKETING
What sort of marketing or advertising do you intend to do?

7 PREMISES/MACHINERY/VEHICLES
Where do you intend to locate the business and why?
What sort and size of premises will you need?
What machinery/vehicles do you require?

8 OBJECTIVES
What objectives do you have for the business?
Short-term
Medium-term
Long-term

International Trade

KEY VOCABULARY

International trade can be defined as the exchange of goods and services between different countries. Depending on what a country produces or needs, it can either **export** (send goods to another country) or **import** (bring in goods from another country).

Governments can control international trade in different ways. The most common measures taken are **tariffs** (or **duties**) and **quotas**. A tariff is a tax imposed on imported goods, whereas a quota is the maximum quantity of a product that may be admitted in a country during a certain period of time. These measures are said to be **protectionist** in that they raise the price of imported goods so that domestically produced goods will gain a price advantage.

The purpose of international organisations, such as GATT (General Agreement on Tariffs and Trade) or EFTA (European Free Trade Association) is to regulate tariffs and to reduce trade restrictions between member countries.

LEAD-IN

1 You will hear an economist from the Organisation for Economic Co-operation and Development (OECD) explaining why countries trade. Listen and answer the following questions.

1 What does the speaker compare countries to?

2 What activity does he give as an example?

3 Why does it make sense for countries to trade?

2 The European Community (EC) was founded in 1957 in order to create a common market in which tariffs and quotas between member countries would be progressively eliminated. Since that date, many steps have been taken to create a single European market, free of all physical, technical and fiscal barriers. With over 300 million people, this single domestic market is the world's largest trading block.

Look at the following list of EC members. Have any countries joined since the list was compiled?

Belgium	Greece	Netherlands
Denmark	Ireland	Portugal
France	Italy	Spain
Germany	Luxemburg	UK

How much do you know about these twelve countries? Working with a partner, see how many questions in the following 'Europe Quiz' you can answer correctly.

1 Which country has the largest area?

2 Which country has the highest population?

3 Which country has the highest birth rate?

4 Which country is the most densely populated?

5 To which EC country does France export the most?

6 To which EC country does Germany export the most?

7 To which EC country does the USA export the most?

8 Which country exports the most . . .
    a crude oil?   **b** cereals?   **c** iron and steel?   **d** citrus fruits?

9 Per inhabitant, which country consumes the most . . .
    a cheese?   **b** sugar?   **c** wine?   **d** cigarettes?

10 Per inhabitant, which country consumes the least . . .
    a cheese?   **b** sugar?   **c** wine?   **d** cigarettes?

11 Which country uses the most nuclear power as a source of energy?

12 Which country has the most magazines?

13 In which country do women play the most active role in the workforce?

14 Which country offers the longest paid holidays?

15 In which country can one find the headquarters of the European company with the highest turnover?

The Spanish oracle

José Luengo has his finger on the pulse of Spanish trade with the UK. His experience of the marketplace has led to importers and exporters seeking his advice before making business deals. Keely Harrison talks to him at his offices in London.

A well-thumbed tome of market statistics sits on the desk and the wall is lined with books on EC regulations, import details and trade information.

This corner of London's Spanish Embassy is the nucleus of Spain's Foreign Trade Inspection and supervision office in the UK, and José Luengo is the sole inspector. He ensures his country's standards and EC guidelines for all imports are met, and feeds information back to Spain on the UK's needs.

Importers and exporters are constantly in contact, seeking his advice on the strawberry market or how current weather in Britain could affect sales of iceberg lettuce. Liaison with quality control laboratories in Spain is also essential to keep up to date with latest developments.

His work covers all imports, from food and drink to animal feeds and industrial goods, but 'the principal task here is with fresh fruit and vegetables, which take up 90% of my time.

'I have to know daily what the prices are here and in other countries. Because we are not fully in the EC there has to be application of levies for produce which goes over quotas. For example, if the price of courgettes in France goes down, we in Spain have to pay a levy.'

The fax and telefax are Mr Luengo's lifelines to Spain and each day he has to fax his opinion on the movements of the marketplace in Europe and in the UK to the Spanish ministry and the exporters' federations.

Except for administration staff, Mr Luengo carries out his work single-handedly, often phoning his counterparts in Germany, where he worked for five years, for moral support and to find out their opinions on the market.

He is something of an oracle, spending much of his time helping exporters with quota problems and advising them to either stop sending certain produce if there is a bumper crop elsewhere in Europe, or face quotas.

'For example, last week weather here in Britain was not good for salads and there was too much on the market. Exporters had to stop sending or put on quotas. We decided to have quotas controlled by the authorities in Spain.'

Total Spanish food and drink imports are currently worth £438m; 731,914 tonnes of fresh fruit and vegetables come into the UK each year.

Because Spain is in a 10-year trial period as a member of the European Community it faces tough measures on exports to other EC countries. By 1995 it will become a fully-fledged member and have the same rights.

'When we signed the treaty with the EC, Europe was more afraid of our potential to export than in reality was necessary,' explains Mr Luengo. 'This is because, firstly, consumption of fresh fruit and vegetables is limited, and secondly, because labour costs in Spain are increasing with our development and in some cases the costs are so high it is not profitable to export to Europe.'

He predicts that with the advent of free trade in 1993, Spain will be fully accepted into the community and its exports not penalised by duties.

UK retailers could then see more price competition between Spanish, French and Dutch produce, particularly on premium products like strawberries, broccoli and aubergines.

Mr Luengo believes full entry into the EC will firm the bond between Spain and the UK with joint ventures between companies wishing to export English summer vegetables to Spain, and import Spanish vegetables during our winter.

There could also be opportunities for UK importers of fresh produce by joining forces with exporters of canned or frozen fruit and vegetables. 'If the price is good the housewife will buy fresh, but if not she buys frozen,' he says.

Mr Luengo believes the quality of Spanish produce has improved greatly during the past three years, particularly in aubergines and courgettes, and thinks the high standards of our supermarkets have encouraged Spanish growers to pursue that quality.

But he believes the key to importing to the UK is 'knowing what this country demands – it is not only a question of price'.

VALUE OF FOOD AND DRINKS (IN £000'S) IMPORTED FROM SPAIN IN THE THREE MONTHS ENDED MARCH 1991

Meat and meat preparations	£1,779
Dairy products and birds' eggs	£219
Fish, crustaceans, molluscs	£3,136
Cereals and cereal preparations	£11,944
Vegetables and fruit	£95,939
Sugar, sugar preparations and honey	£859
Coffee, tea, cocoa, spices	£2,231
Beverages	£18,969

Source: Department of Trade and Industry

Super Marketing

READING

Read the text and choose the best answers for each question.

1 Which of the following is **not** one of Mr Luengo's duties?
  a Providing advice to importers and exporters.
  b Ensuring that EC regulations for imports are respected.
  c Setting export quotas.

2 Because Spain is not yet a full member of the EC,
  a it can only export fruit and vegetables.
  b controls are imposed on its exports to other EC countries.
  c its exports are not penalised by duties.

3 Which of the following statements is false according to the article?
  a In the future, there will be more joint ventures between Spain and the UK.
  b Labour costs in Spain are decreasing.
  c The quality of Spanish produce has improved during the past few years.

4 According to Mr Luengo, in order to export to the UK, you must be particularly attentive to:
  a price
  b labour costs
  c demand

5 According to the table at the end of the article, which Spanish product does the UK import the lowest quantity of?
  a milk, butter and eggs
  b fruit and vegetables
  c wine and beverages

VOCABULARY

Work with a partner to complete the crossword. The answers are all in the text.

CLUES

Across

1 exchange of goods or services
3 decreases (4-4)
8 a person who belongs to an organisation
10 a place where goods are bought and sold
11 possessive adjective
12 official advice about how to do something
14 past participle of *meet*
16 trade restrictions
18 a machine for transmitting messages
19 work
22 A _____ venture is when two companies work together for a common cause.
24 United Kingdom
26 communication and co-operation between different sections of an organisation
27 admission
28 a tax on imported goods

29 without restrictions
30 A _____ period is an experimental period.

Down

2 to require, to need
4 a piece of office furniture, like a table
5 to the value of
6 a rule
7 purchases
9 legal entitlements
10 a government department
13 the people who work for an organisation
15 a formal agreement between two or more countries
17 a person or company that sells goods abroad
20 If you give someone _____, you tell them what they should do.
21 one and only
23 as well as; also
25 something that helps you to understand or solve a problem

THE INVOICE

In the context of international trade, the invoice provides information about the goods exchanged between the exporter and the importer. This document is prepared by the exporter and includes a description of the goods, their price and the quantity supplied.

Look at the following invoice and the explanation of the information it contains. Then listen to the cassette and complete the missing numbers, dates and amounts.

METROPOLITAN TENNIS EQUIPMENT COMPANY
4019 Beach Boulevard South
Los Angeles, California 90126
Telephone: 615.890.9000
Fax: 615.890.9077 — Exporter's name and address

Champion Sport Ltd. — Importer's name and address
71 Victoria Lane
St John's Wood
London NW1 3PP

Date .... (1) — Date of issue

Invoice No.................................. (2)

QUANTITY	DESCRIPTION	AMOUNT	
.... (3)	Tennis Rackets .... (4) of 'GX12' model .... (5) of 'Tennis Pro' model		
	Ex-works price: GX12 model £78 each Tennis Pro model £116 each	£........	.... (6)
	All freight charges and export packing	£........	.... (7)
	Insurance from warehouse to warehouse	£........	.... (8)
	C.I.F. London Total	£........	.... (9)
Marks & Nos.	.... (10) cardboard cartons – .... (11) per carton		
	Import Licence No. .... (12)		
MET CS LTD LONDON 1-16	per pro Metropolitan Tennis Equipment *Robert Morales.*		

Description of the goods

Cost of freight and insurance (if specifically requested)

Total amount payable

Shipment terms. C.I.F. = cost, insurance and freight. The port of destination is named.

Number and type of packages
The contents of individual packages

The export and/or import licence numbers

Marks and numbers on packages

Signature of the exporter

LANGUAGE FOCUS

MODAL VERBS: OBLIGATION

Look at the following sentences from the text:

'I have to know daily what the prices are ...' (line 28)

'... each day he has to fax his opinion on the movements of the marketplace in Europe ...' (line 36)

In both these examples, the modal verb *have to* is used to express an obligation. What meaning do the following verbs express? Complete the table.

have to	should/shouldn't	ought to	don't have to
needn't	must/mustn't	need to	don't need to

obligation or necessity	*have to* ....
mild obligation or advice	....
absence of obligation or necessity	....

➤➤ For more information on modal verbs, turn to page 157.

Practice

1 Below you will find a list of advice to clothes exporters on how best to approach the German retail market. Read each piece of advice and write a summary sentence using the verbs above.

Example: Buyers in the German retail trade are known for their professionalism. They have a reputation for being demanding but are fair with people who are as professional as they are.

When dealing with the Germans you must be professional.

1 Avoid turning up unexpectedly for meetings with German buyers. It is always better to arrange an advance appointment, preferably by telephone.

2 German buyers are constantly looking for collections with a strong profile: it is not the size of the collection that counts. On the contrary, the more compact the collection, the more it will attract the buyer's attention.

3 The quality of your product is extremely important. This is what buyers will be most interested in.

4 German buyers tend to give precise delivery dates, for example 25 January 1993. That is the date for delivery – not the day before and not the day after. Good delivery performance is therefore essential.

5 A letter of credit is a convenient and secure way of arranging for payment, but it is by no means the only method.

6 Never produce handwritten price lists in foreign currencies. Type your prices out neatly and present them in Deutschmarks.

7 When dealing with German companies it is a good idea to employ an agent to work for you, although this is not essential.

2 An American delegation from your company's head office will be visiting your country during the entire month of December. You have been asked to help write a short practical guide which will be distributed to the members of the delegation before they leave. Using the categories below, make a list of the advice that you would give.

documents	what to bring	leisure activities	shopping
language	food and drink	health and safety	tipping

Example: *You have to have a visa in order to enter the country.*

DESCRIBING TRENDS

Unit 1 looked at some of the nouns and verbs used to describe changes in price, quantity and amount, for example:

Noun	Verb
an increase	to increase
a rise	to rise
a decrease	to decrease
a drop	to drop
a fall	to fall

These can be qualified with an adjective or adverb to describe a change more precisely.

Practice

1 Complete the table.

	Adjective	Adverb
Used to show a regular movement:	steady gradual	
Used to show a small change:	slight	
Used to show considerable, striking or unexpected change:	sharp dramatic sudden	

2 Use an appropriate adjective or adverb to complete the descriptions of the following graphs.

Prices

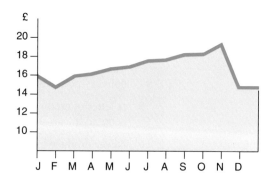

Prices rose [1]............................ from February to October, before falling [2]............................ in November.

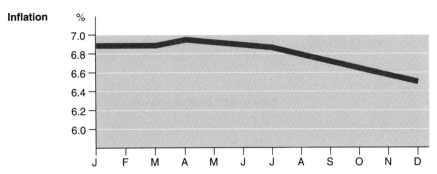

Inflation rose [3]........................... in March, before beginning its [4]........................... descent to today's figure of 6.5%.

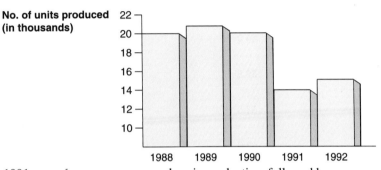

1991 saw a [5]........................... drop in production, followed by a [6]........................... recovery in 1992.

3 Here are some other expressions which are used to describe trends. Which parts of the following graph would you use them to talk about?

to fluctuate	to level off	to remain stable
to reach a peak	to stand at . . .	

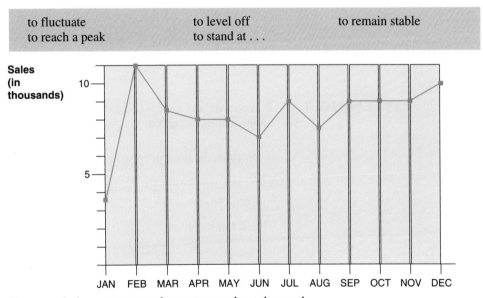

Now match these parts to make sentences about the graph.

1	Sales reached a peak	**a**	10,000 in December.
2	Sales fluctuated	**b**	from September to November.
3	Sales remained stable	**c**	of 11,000.
4	Sales stood at	**d**	at about 8,000 in April.
5	Sales levelled off	**e**	from May to September.

SKILLS FOCUS

WRITING   Study the following graph, then write a short description of the evolution of New Zealand wool prices between 1965 and 1985.

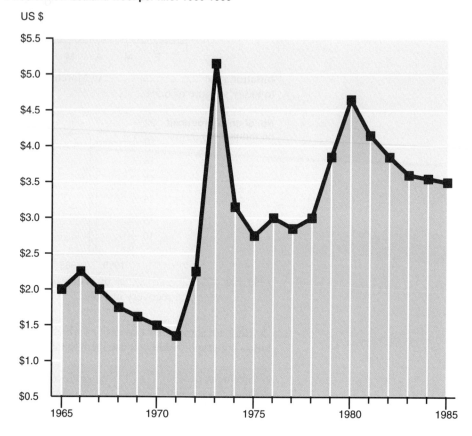

Price of New Zealand wool per kilo: 1965-1985

LISTENING 1   **1** You will hear a speaker commenting on the graph you have just studied. Listen and complete the description.

> In 1965, the price of New Zealand wool [1]............................ $1.98 per kilo. It then
> [2]............................ by 20 cents in 1966 before falling [3]............................ to $1.37 in
> 1971. There was a [4]............................ increase over the next two years, with the
> price of wool [5]............................ of $5.13 in 1973. From 1974 to 1978 the price
> [6]............................ between a high of $3.20 and a low of $2.75, before
> [7]............................ $4.60 in 1980. After falling again to $3.60 in 1983, the price
> [8]............................ at $3.55 in 1985.

Examine the similarities and differences between your description and the one above.

2 You will now hear descriptions of the production of coal, crude steel and wine in three different European countries from 1985 to 1990. Listen and complete the following graphs.

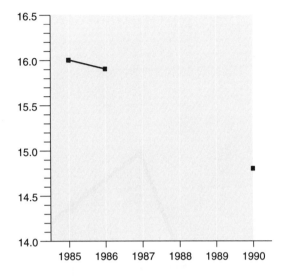

1 **Production of Coal – Spain**
   1985-1990 (in millions of metric tons)

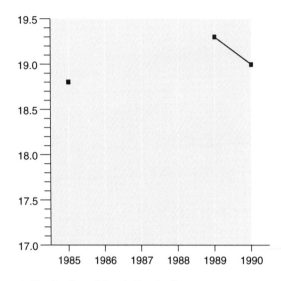

2 **Production of Crude Steel – France**
   1985-1990 (in millions of metric tons)

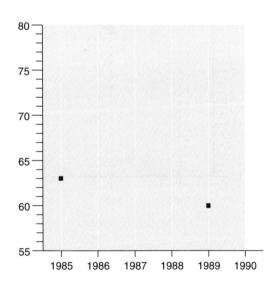

3 **Production of Wine – Italy**
   1985-1990 (in millions of hectolitres)

SPEAKING   **1** Work in groups of four. You are each going to study a graph showing the exports of wheat for one of four different countries. Look at the following pages:

Student A … page 126   Student C … page 149

Student B … page 147   Student D … page 151

Student A

The graph below shows the USA's wheat exports for the period 1985-1990. Describe the information to your colleagues. Then listen to their descriptions and complete the graph for all four countries using the following key.

- - - - - - - - Canada   ┼┼┼┼┼┼ EC   ●━●━●━● Australia

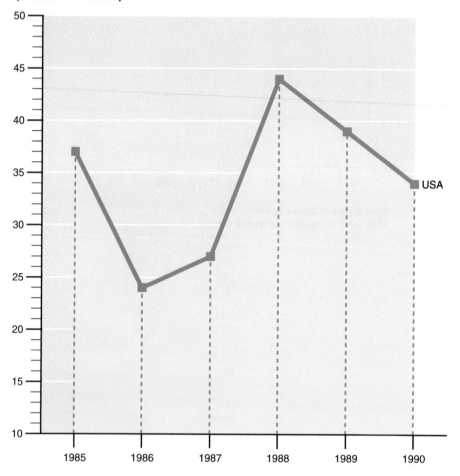

Wheat Exports 1985-1990 (in millions of tonnes)

2 As a group you should now answer the following questions using the information you have obtained.

1 Which of the four countries exported the most wheat over the six-year period?

2 Which country exported the lowest amount of wheat in 1986?

3 How many tonnes of wheat did Canada export in 1989?

4 What was the best year for wheat exports?

5 Which two countries exported identical quantities of wheat in the same year? In which year did this happen?

6 In which years did the EC export more wheat than Canada?

7 Which country's wheat exports appear to be in steady decline?

LISTENING 2

1 You will hear an economist from the OECD talking about protectionism. Listen and decide whether the following statements are true or false.

	T	F
1 Government decisions about protectionism are often influenced by interest groups.		
2 According to the speaker, protectionism creates jobs.		
3 The argument for protectionism appears to be attractive.		
4 Protectionism encourages people to be efficient.		
5 According to the speaker, the United States should stop importing Japanese cars.		

2 You will now hear the speaker talking about the European Community's Common Agricultural Policy (CAP). Listen and note down what he says about the effects it has on the following:

EC farmers and producers

....
....
....

EC food prices

....
....
....

EEC production

....
....
....

EC's trading partners

....
....
....

Insurance

KEY VOCABULARY

People buy insurance to protect themselves against the losses that may result from an accident or catastrophe. For example, a company involved in a major construction project may have all the necessary skills for completing the job but there is still an element of **risk**. Extreme weather conditions or a natural disaster could damage or destroy the work that has been done. To protect itself, the company can pay a sum of money – a **premium** – to an **insurance company** who will **underwrite** the risk or guarantee to provide financial **compensation** if such an event occurs. The exact details of this insurance are contained in the **insurance policy** which is a document showing the risks that have been **insured against** and the levels of compensation that will be paid.

LEAD-IN

You will hear six people describing the principal risks that they face. Listen and identify the type of risk that each person is most likely to insure against. Choose from the following:

theft	burglary	personal injury
breakage	fire	third party

1 ....   4 ....

2 ....   5 ....

3 ....   6 ....

READING

1 Read the text on the opposite page and decide to which group or groups the following statements refer. The first one has been done for you.

	Insurance Companies	Lloyd's of London	Insurance Brokers
1 They provide a major reinsurance market.	✓	✓	
2 They deal with most of the UK company business.			
3 They earn almost £1 billion per week in premium income.			
4 They help people to choose the best insurance.			
5 They originally provided insurance for ships.			
6 They do most of their business abroad.			
7 They can be small operations managed by just one person.			
8 They cover many different types of risk.			

Insurance Services

London is a leading centre for international insurance.

The industry in the UK is broadly made up of three groups – insurance companies, Lloyd's of London and insurance brokers.

The insurance companies and Lloyd's 5 combined provide a major reinsurance market. London's importance as an insurance centre, as well as its comparative freedom from excessive regulation, has attracted many foreign reinsurance companies and brokers.

10 *Insurance Companies*

There are around 850 insurance companies authorised in the UK but approximately one half of them handle more than 90% of company market 15 business. They provide the full range of insurance contracts including life, pensions, permanent health insurance, marine, aviation, fire, accident, motor, travel and household insurance.

20 The insurance companies have a combined premium income of more than £50 billion per year.

Lloyd's of London

Lloyd's is a unique international insurance 25 market. Lloyd's is a society of underwriters made up of more than 26,000 members or 'names' who as private individuals, accept insurance risks and are liable for claims to the full extent of their personal wealth.

30 The Members are grouped in some 350 syndicates. Business is introduced by Lloyd's broking firms – there are some 240 of them –

who look for the best quotation on behalf of their clients.

35 Although its origins lie with marine insurance, Lloyd's now covers almost any risk, from oil refineries, aircraft, road vehicles and satellites – even to a wine taster's palate.

More than three-quarters of this business 40 originates from overseas and its premium income is approximately £24 million every day.

Lloyd's of London

Insurance Brokers

Brokers or intermediaries look for the best cover for their clients and offer advice on 45 insurance. Their size can range from a simple one-man operation to a City-based international broker with a turnover running into millions.

Brokers place their business with the 50 insurance companies and – if they are accredited – with Lloyd's. Brokers handle approximately 70% of the general United Kingdom insurance business.

British Invisibles, Corporation of London

---

2 Read the text again and decide if the following statements are true or false:

	T	F
1 Any insurance broker can place business with Lloyd's of London.		
2 Lloyd's guarantees to provide cover for almost all risks.		
3 The insurance companies handle more business than Lloyd's.		
4 A Member of Lloyd's has limited financial liability.		
5 The London insurance market attracts little foreign business.		

3 In which of the categories of insurance listed in paragraph 3 would the following be included?

VOCABULARY

1 Find words in the text to describe the people who do the following:

1 act as intermediaries and offer advice to customers about insurance ....

2 invest in the Lloyd's syndicates as private individuals ....

3 buy a service ....

2 Match the words from the text with their corresponding definitions.

1 reinsurance (*line 5*)

2 life (*line 16*)

3 premium income (*line 21*)

4 society (*line 25*)

5 claim (*line 28*)

6 syndicate (*line 31*)

7 quotation (*line 33*)

8 cover (*line 36*)

9 the City (*line 46*)

a a request for compensation from someone who is insured

b the amount of money that an insurance company receives in payments from its customers

c protection through insurance

d the price at which an insurer would be prepared to accept a risk

e a category of insurance related to the inevitability of death

f an association of people with common interests

g the financial centre of London

h a group of Lloyd's members who work as a unit

i a way for insurers to reduce their own risks by placing some of their business with other insurers

3 Complete the following passage, using words from Exercises 1 and 2, and from the Key Vocabulary section at the beginning of this unit. Change the form of the words where necessary.

> Roger Hartfield has recently applied to become a ¹............................. of a Lloyd's ²............................. . This means that he will have to prove that he has a minimum of £250,000 in capital which can be used as a guarantee for the ³............................. that his representatives at Lloyd's will ⁴............................. . If the income from the ⁵............................. of the customers who insure themselves with his group exceeds the amount of money that has to be paid out in ⁶............................. then Roger Hartfield will make a profit. However, if that is not the case, he may have to sell his house and personal possessions in order to provide them with the necessary ⁷............................. .

DISCUSSION

Look at the following list of people and items insured on the Lloyd's insurance market. Discuss the potential risks which are involved in each case, using a modal of possibility (*may/might/could*).

Example: The 286 Sainsbury supermarkets in the UK
- *There **may** be a fire in a store.*
- *A shopper or an employee **might** have an accident outside or inside a store.*
- *The products sold by the store **could** be faulty.*

1 Michael Jackson, Elton John and Rod Stewart

2 The Van Gogh art exhibition in Amsterdam

3 The world's largest cigar, twelve and a half feet long and weighing 110 kgs

4 A £1 million prize offered by Cutty Sark Whisky to anyone who can capture the Loch Ness monster

5 The beards of the 40 members of the 'Whiskers Club' in Derbyshire in England

6 The outdoor opera festival in the Italian city of Verona

LANGUAGE FOCUS

EXPRESSING APPROXIMATION

The following words can all be used to express approximation:

about	approximately	around
nearly	roughly	some

Look at these examples from the text:

*There are **around** 850 insurance companies authorised in the UK but **approximately** one half of them handle more than 90% of company market business.* (para. 3)

*The Members are grouped in **some** 350 syndicates. Business is introduced by Lloyd's broking firms – there are **some** 240 of them – who look for the best quotation on behalf of their clients.* (para. 6)

Can you find any more examples?

Practice

Prudential Corporation plc is one of the world's largest life insurance groups.

Working with a partner, comment on the following figures, using an expression of approximation.

Example: *Prudential Corporation employs about 30,000 people worldwide.*

Prudential Corporation plc: Information at 31 December 1991	
No of employees (worldwide):	29,886
No. of employees (UK):	25,886
No. of customers (worldwide):	8.3 million
Funds under management:	£50.9 billion
Dividend per share:	11.0 pence
Premium income from long term business:	£6.01 billion
Profit made before tax:	£267 million

LISTENING

Don Raley

SKILLS FOCUS

1 You will hear Don Raley, an expert in the field of insurance, talking about the way that Lloyd's operates. Listen and take notes under the following headings:

■ Syndicates
■ Underwriters
■ Brokers
■ Names

2 Listen to the second extract.

1 According to Don Raley, what three advantages does Lloyd's have over the insurance companies?

2 How has it managed to achieve these advantages?

3 Now listen again and find the words that the speaker uses to mean the following:

a strong points ....

b been unable ....

c the cost of running a business ....

d eliminating ....

e to minimise ....

f in the area of ....

g experts ....

3 In the final extract Don Raley talks about changes in the way that Lloyd's operates.

1 Listen and select the key words that he uses to describe the changes in the following areas:

a Liability ....
....

b Regulation ....
....

c Marketing ....
....

2 Why does Don Raley think change is necessary?

3 Listen again. In which of the three areas above are changes already happening? In which are changes planned?

SPEAKING

Evaluating risk

1 Work in small groups. Read the following document which describes the main criteria that are used by UK insurers to define a standard driver who would pay the normal rate for motor insurance cover.

Any exceptions would probably result in the driver paying a higher premium. Would you qualify for the normal rate? If not, how many conditions would you fail on?

The Driver

The person seeking insurance must:

■ be the main user of the car.

■ be between the ages of 25 and 74.

■ have been resident in the UK for at least 3 years.

■ have had a full UK driving licence for the past 12 months.

■ have had no motoring convictions during the past 3 years.

■ have had no suspension of licence during the past 5 years.

■ have had no motor insurance containing special terms or increased premiums.

■ not have a physical defect, infirmity or suffer from a heart condition or diabetes.

■ not be engaged in the following businesses or occupations:
   Casino, Night Club, Disc Jockey, Musician, Professional sport, Entertainment, Show Business, Student.

Another factor used in determining the premium that will be charged for motor insurance is what is called the 'group rating'. Under this system each model of car is included in one of twenty groups depending on a variety of factors such as:

■ Cost of spare parts
■ Repair times
■ Price of the car
■ Performance
■ Car security and anti-theft features

The classification of a particular model will therefore indicate the risks that the insurer is exposed to. In the UK, for example, a Mini would be included in the lowest group and a Ferrari in the highest.

2 On the opposite page you will find three forms which have been completed by three people who wish to insure their cars. Read these forms carefully and then, using the information you have just studied, discuss what you think are the characteristics of each of these risks, putting yourselves in the position of an underwriter.

WRITING

Write a short report explaining how you evaluated each of the application forms, and stating which of them you would be prepared to accept as an insurance risk and under what conditions.

Application for motor insurance

#	Question	Form 1	Form 2	Form 3
1	Full name:	Zaniewski Jules	George Brown	Peter Campbell
2	Address:	c/o Clarendon Hotel, Beechwood Road, London	100 High Street, Newton ABB 120	6 Main Street, Buigliton, Anglia Q21 77B
3	Date of birth:	22/10/1940	20.4.35	26/2/41
4	Occupation:	Art Dealer	Bank Manager	Building Contractor
5	Date UK/EC driving test passed:	1971 (USA)	1959	1968
6	Vehicle make and model:	BMW 520i	Volkswagen Golf GTi	Ford Escort L
7	Engine size:	2494	1588	1298
8	Year of manufacture:	1991	1990	1991
9	Present value:	£77,000	£8,200	£5,900
10	Who will be the principal user?	J. Zaniewski	G. Brown & M. Brown	Peter Campbell
11	Where is the vehicle garaged?	Clarendon Hotel	At above address	6 Main Street, Buigliton
12	No. of years of no-claims bonuses:		None	6 years
13	Will the vehicle be used for business purposes?		No	No
14	Give details of other persons, who will or may drive the car:			
a	Name:		Mary Brown, John Brown	Emma Campbell
b	Date of birth:		22.10.36, 21.1.75	6.10.1948
c	Date UK/EC driving test passed:		1965, 1991	1972
15	Have you or any person who will drive the car:			
a	been involved in a motor accident in the last three years?	Yes	No	Yes
b	been convicted of any motoring offences in the past five years?	Yes	No	No
c	ever suffered from any physical or mental infirmity?	Yes	No	Yes
d	ever been refused insurance or had special terms imposed?	No	No	Yes
e	been resident in the UK for less than 3 years?	Yes	No	No

* If you have answered yes to any of these questions please give full details in the space provided:

Form 1: a) collided with motorcycle in Dec. 1991

b) driving without due care and attention (1991). Fined £200.

Form 3: a) Emma Campbell 2 minor accidents – collided with post whilst reversing car – struck car whilst parking (no claims made) c) P. Campbell lost sight of left eye 10 years ago. d) Paid extra insurance premium for disability imposed four years ago.

Signature: *J. Zaniewski*   *George Brown*   *Peter Campbell*

Corporate Identity

KEY VOCABULARY

The term **corporate identity** refers to the image that a company creates for itself and presents to its public. It can include everything from the way the receptionist answers the phone, to the design of its offices or retail outlets, to the way it carries out its advertising. It is especially important for large companies with diverse activities to produce a standard corporate identity programme, to ensure that they project a coherent and positive image in all their markets. Visually, a company's identity is represented by its **logo** – the graphic symbol by which the company is known.

LEAD-IN

1 The following factors all play a part in creating a company's identity. Choose two companies from your country and say which of these contribute the most to forming the opinion you have of them. Report your findings to the class.

- its products or services
- its staff
- its buildings (interior and exterior)
- its philosophy
- its advertising
- its logo
- its management style

2 When companies want to make their products known to the public, they can plan a product advertising campaign. Likewise, when they want to inform the public about the way they run their companies or about their policies and philosophy in general, they can do so through corporate advertising.

Look at the corporate advertisement on the opposite page. Working with a partner, discuss the following questions.

1 What facts do you learn about the company from the advertisement?

2 What attitudes or feelings do you have toward the company after reading the advertisement?

3 In the copy (or text), which words are used to give you positive feelings toward the company?

4 What type of image is BP trying to project through this advertisement?

Present your findings to the class.

Thanks to BP solar lighting, Colin's future looks considerably brighter.

Colin can read by sunlight even after the sun has gone down.

Colin lives in a remote African village. He has no light to study by at home, so after a full day of classes he remains at school to finish his homework.

You may wonder where he gets the energy. Actually it comes in the form of electricity generated by solar modules.

Since 1981 we've supplied solar-powered vaccine refrigerators and water pumps to clinics, and lighting systems to schools throughout the African continent.

Solar technology may never eclipse conventional power sources. But it already promises the children of Africa a brighter future.

Supplying solar power to remote parts of the world is one of the things BP is doing today, for all our tomorrows.

For all our tomorrows.

READING

BP is a leading international petroleum and petrochemical company. Its main sectors of activity are oil and gas exploration, production, refining and marketing. Due to its increasing international presence, and following several acquisitions made by the company, BP decided to adopt a new, more dynamic look and at the same time to redesign their logo to reflect this change of image. The text opposite describes how the decisions were made.

1 Five sentences have been removed from the text – you will find them below. Read the text and insert each sentence in its appropriate position.

A Our image is a major commercial and political asset; like any asset it has to be managed and looked after.

B BP's corporate image is therefore how BP's many publics regard the company.

C These were then tested on members of the public in street polls and in special discussion groups.

D The Image Study Group was therefore established at corporate level, with representatives from major businesses and associates.

E There followed an international market research programme to test public perceptions of BP.

2 Read the text again in more detail and answer the following questions.

1 Why did BP set up an Image Study Group?

2 What did BP instruct the Image Study Group to do?

3 What did it reveal about the staff's attitude towards the company?

4 What did it reveal about the public's attitude towards the company?

5 What conclusions did the Image Study Group reach?

6 Why, according to David Walton, is a company's image so important?

VOCABULARY

1 Match the words from the text with their corresponding definitions.

1 brand (*line 25*)		**a**	superiority over other companies
2 brief (*line 37*)		**b**	something that is useful or valuable
3 stand for (*line 52*)		**c**	a particular make of a product
4 perception (*line 64*)		**d**	an opinion formed through observation
5 carry out (*line 65*)		**e**	a survey of public opinion
6 impact (*line 76*)		**f**	dedication and devotion to achieving objectives
7 poll (*line 82*)		**g**	to represent
8 commitment (*line 95*)		**h**	a strong effect or impression
9 competitive advantage (*line 97*)		**i**	a precise description of a job to be done
10 asset (*line 107*)		**j**	to do or complete (a task)

How the decisions were made

A year-long corporate image study posed the vital questions:

- How do we see ourselves?
- How do others see us?
- What image should we adopt for the 1990s?

Image is now a much used, and often misused, word. It is how others see us. **1**..

BP's identity is what we are and what we do to form that image; it is what we stand for.

So behind the decision to adopt a fresh identity lay an intensive study which examined the very nature of the present BP group and what its present image is. The devolution of the group into separate businesses, and a stream of acquisitions, had meant profound changes to its structure.

A fundamental review of BP's identities, images and brands was decided upon to ensure we obtained the best blend of corporate business and national images throughout the world. **2**.. It was jointly led by David Walton, General Manager of BP's Government and Public Affairs Department and the Chief Executive of BP Oil International, initially James Ross and then Russell Seal.

The Image Study's brief was to examine the nature of the changes in the group and what they meant both to staff and the world at large. Having established how BP was viewed today, decisions were taken about the kind of image we wanted to project and whether the present logo and the general style of the group accurately reflected that image.

The Study Group began by inviting senior managers from businesses and associates worldwide to submit their views as to what BP stood for.

The survey revealed that staff felt we should project ourselves as more dynamic, innovative, international and better related to the customer. These tougher business aims were tempered by a strong feeling that the company should also be seen to be a good employer and socially responsible, working today for all our tomorrows. **3**.. Surveys were carried out in the United Kingdom, Germany, the United States, Singapore and Australia. External views of BP were in many ways similar to those of employees: that we should harness technology for the future while maintaining a responsible attitude to society and the environment.

It was an essential exercise to examine the impact of both evolutionary and more radical types of logo. To this end designers in Europe and the United States worked independently to come up with a wide range of ideas. **4**..

The result of the year-long study was to confirm the need for a fresh new style but one based on our well known symbol of excellence and integrity, the BP shield.

David Walton summarised the essence of the Image Study in this way; 'A properly managed, cohesive, professional and distinctive identity is important both internally and externally, because it signals commitment and purpose, commands respect and gives competitive advantage. That is why this new development is so vital for our company.

'As chairman of the new Identity Committee which has been established to ensure the effective working of the new identity and brand management system, it is my responsibility to make certain of success. **5**... I hope and expect that everyone will find the new approach effective and relevant in their business lives.'

2 Complete the following passage using words from exercise 1.

> As more and more companies selling the same product come onto the market, our company realised that our current product advertising was no longer enough to ensure us a ¹............................ . We decided to ²............................ a market study to discover what ³............................ people had of the company and its products. We organised a ⁴............................ to find out what the public thought our company should ⁵............................ . The results showed that people needed to view the company as an organisation with a ⁶............................ to worthwhile objectives. Therefore we organised a corporate advertising campaign showing the company as a caring member of the community. We haven't been able to measure the ⁷............................ of the campaign yet.

3 Go through paragraphs 6 and 10 of the text and make a list of adjectives used to describe BP's image. Then using a dictionary, match these words to their opposites provided below.

1 local or regional ....

2 immobile or static ....

3 amateurish or unbusinesslike ....

4 backward or old-fashioned ....

5 badly defined or not clear ....

6 undependable or uncaring ....

7 common or ordinary ....

DISCUSSION

Below and on the opposite page you will find a selection of BP advertisements from the past. Study them carefully and say in each case what image of the product is being portrayed. Compare these ads to the corporate ad in the Lead-in section and comment on the difference in content and message between the advertisements.

LANGUAGE FOCUS

THE ARTICLE

The following nouns are from the BP advertisement on page 137. Read the advertisement again and identify which form of the article is used with each noun: the definite article (*the*), the indefinite article (*a/an*), or no article. Can you explain why?

sunlight	sun	village	home
energy	electricity	children	world

➤➤ For more information on the article, turn to page 157.

Practice

1 Complete the following passage, putting in the correct form of the article where necessary.

In February 1990, Perrier, one of [1]............ most famous mineral water companies, faced [2]............ serious image problem when small quantities of benzene were found in some bottles. [3]............ company decided to take 160 million bottles worth $70 million off the market. [4]............ spokesperson from [5]............ communications department made [6]............ statement to the press saying that this did not present [7]............ health problem, but he did admit that for [8]............ product known for purity, it was definitely [9].......... mistake. [10]............ independent environmental consultant carried out [11]............ inspection at the Perrier plant and identified and corrected [12]............ fault. [13]............ same consultant said that a person spilling one drop of [14]............ lead-free petrol on their hand would absorb more benzene than if they drank a bottle of Perrier every day for a year. In this instance Perrier's policy of [15]............ honesty and its concern for [16]............ consumers saved its image and good name.

SKILLS FOCUS

LISTENING

You will hear an interview with Glenn Tuttsel, Creative Director of Michael Peters Ltd., a design consultancy based in London.

1 In this first extract, Glenn Tuttsel talks about the two areas of corporate identity design in which his company is involved. Listen and complete the following table.

Area of design:	Existing company (re-design)	New company (new identity)

Problem:	Present identity:
	● may be [1].................................
	● may no longer be relevant,
	  e.g. if the company is going
	  to [2].................................
		New identity needs to become
		[3].................................... in a
		short space of time.

Initial role of design consultancy:	● carries out in-depth research into a) what the company wants to be
	  b) [4].................................
	● works with the [5].................................. to create a brief for the
	  new corporate identity design. This is done by interviewing:
	a) [6].................................
	b) customers
	c) [7].................................	

2 Look at the photos illustrating the old and new logos for the BBC and Associated Tyre Specialists. Then listen to the second extract and take notes under the following headings.

	Problem of old identity	**Solution**
BBC		
ATS		

SPEAKING 1

1 Many companies sponsor events to maintain their image or to create a new image. Sponsorship can cover a whole range of activities including sport, education, conservation of the environment and local community projects. The activity or event chosen depends on the type of image the company wants to project, for example, IBM contributes computers to business schools in The United States and Coca-Cola gives financial aid to black students who want to become teachers.

Working in pairs, make a list of as many companies as you can think of which sponsor one or more of the activities mentioned above. Say in each case what kind of image the company wants to project through its sponsorship.

2 Convincing a sponsor

Work in small groups. Choose one of the following projects and imagine that you are looking for sponsorship on its behalf.

1

An international sports event

You are members of a regional chess federation and are organising a world championship chess tournament. Sixteen of the world's best players have been invited to participate. The event will take place at the National Exhibition Hall. You need sponsorship to help pay for the media facilities which you must provide and to cover other expenses such as air fares and accommodation.

2

An international business congress

Every year the business development committee of your town organises an international business congress. The theme chosen for this year's event is 'New trends in business'. Activities will include an exhibition of stands presenting various business projects, conferences with guest speakers from different companies and viewings of in-company, promotion, and recruitment videos.

3

An international exhibition of children's art

You represent the National Art Gallery and are organising an exhibition of children's art from all over the world. You are looking for a sponsor to finance programmes, catalogues, reproductions etc. You have invited a famous artist to open the exhibition, and children and teachers from various countries will be available for a press conference.

4

A TV documentary

You are directors of a video company and you have been commissioned by a national TV network to make a programme about the effects of pollution on marine life in the Pacific, as part of a wildlife series. It is also your job to find a sponsor to finance the highly sophisticated equipment and specialised crew members necessary to make this programme.

One of the companies you have decided to ask for sponsorship is the international computer group, Better Computing International (BCI). Discuss the various advantages that your project can offer BCI and prepare a list of arguments that you will use to persuade them to sponsor you. You should consider the following document which lists some of the questions that a company will ask itself before sponsoring a project. How will your project satisfy the directors of BCI with respect to these questions?

Checklist

1 What is our target audience and does the project match?

2 Will it appeal to our customers?

3 Does the project have a logical link with our company? If not, could one be developed?

4 Is the activity unique or only one of many similar things on offer?

5 Will there be other sponsors? If so, are they our competitors?

6 What kind of media coverage does the project offer? (For example, local press, TV, company name/logo on T-shirts, programmes etc.)

7 What are the chances of the project being successful? (We don't want negative publicity.)

8 If our sponsorship is a success, will there be future opportunities to continue our connection with the activity or event?

9 Does the activity or event present an opportunity to invite our employees or shareholders as observers or participants?

10 Are any of our customers involved directly or indirectly in this activity or event?

WRITING

Working in the same groups, write a letter to BCI asking them to consider your request for sponsorship. Use the model opposite to help you.

SPEAKING 2

Once you have completed your letters to BCI, circulate them amongst the other groups in the class until you have read them all. Consider each letter as if you were directors of BCI. Which project would you choose and why? Present your final decision to the rest of the class.

Your address ———————

Date ———————

Name/job title and address of
person to whom you are writing ———

Opening greeting ——— **Dear Sir/Madam,**

I am a member of a team ... *(give details)* ... **currently working on** ...
(present the project in general terms). **I am contacting you because** ...
(introduce the idea of their possible interest in sponsoring the project) ...

... *(In this second paragraph, you should outline the event giving dates, times and
activities. Give specific reasons why the project should interest your correspondent,
including possible media coverage, customer appeal etc.)* ...

... *(In this closing paragraph, say how you hope the project will be of interest to
your correspondent.)* ...

Closing formalities ——— **Should you require further details, please do not hesitate to
contact me.**

I look forward to hearing from you.

Yours faithfully,

Your signature ——— ———

Communication Activities

Unit 1, page 11

Student B

Read the following profile and be ready to play the role of Giancarlo Peretto. Prepare a list of questions that you will need to ask Susan Robertson (played by Student A) in order to complete her profile. Then take it in turns to interview each other.

Examples: *How long have you been with your present company?*

Name: Giancarlo Peretto

Age: 48

Nationality: Italian

Marital status: Married, 3 children

Salary: $155,000 per annum

Company: The Milan Bank of Commerce

Present position: • Chief Financial Officer
• Reports to the Managing Director

Background: • Studied at the London School of Economics
• Joined the accounts department in 1978

Present responsibilities:
• Leads a team of senior executives working on various aspects of financial management
• In charge of planning the bank's financial strategy

Name: Susan Robertson

Age: ....

Nationality: ....

Marital status: ....

Salary: ....

Company: ....

Present position: ....
....

Background: ....
....

Present responsibilities: ....
....
....
....
....

Unit 1, page 12

Student B

Read the following company profile and study the kind of information it contains. Be prepared to answer questions about it.

Virgin is a leading international company based in London. It was founded in 1970 by Richard Branson, the present Chairman. The group has three main divisions which operate independently. These divisions specialise in music retailing and entertainment, communications and travel. Virgin operates in 15 different countries, including the United States, the United Kingdom, Continental Europe, Australia and Japan. Its sales in 1991 were £1100 million. It employs over 6,000 people.

Now ask your partner questions to obtain similar information about the company that he or she has been working on, and complete the notes below.

Name of company ....

Headquarters ....

Chairman ....

Business activities ....

Main markets ....

Sales in 1990 ....

No. of employees ....

Unit 11, page 103/104

Student B

SPECIFICATIONS	CAR A	CAR B	CAR C
Model		Renault Espace 2.9RXE	
Price		£23,875	
Type of engine		V6	
Engine capacity		2,849 cc	
Power		153 b.h.p.	
Weight		1,359 kg.	
Maximum speed		195 k.p.h.	
Acceleration from 0-100 k.p.h.		10.3 secs	
Petrol consumption (per 100 km) Town driving At 90 k.p.h.		15.4 l. 8.6 l.	
Seating capacity		7	
Additional information		Rearrangeable seats, excellent vision and virtually maintenance free	

Unit 13, page 126

Student B

The graph opposite shows Canada's wheat exports for the period 1985-1990. Describe the information to your colleagues. Then listen to their descriptions and complete the graph for all four countries using the following key.

+++++++ EC

•-•-•-• Australia

———— USA

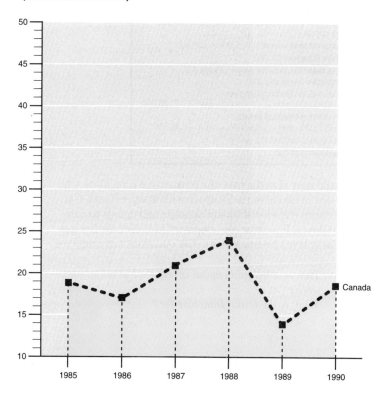

Wheat Exports 1985-1990
(in millions of tonnes)

Unit 3, page 33

Student B:
You are a business person going to negotiate in a foreign country. As part of the preparation for your trip, you have arranged to meet a consultant (Student A), who is an expert on the culture of this country. Using the headings below, draw up a list of the questions that you would ask him/her.

Use of language	Non-verbal communication	Business negotiations	Socialising

Examples:
Do I call my business contact by his/her first name?   *How important is it to exchange business cards in this country?*
How should I greet my business partners?   *Are there any topics to avoid in an informal conversation?*

Unit 5, page 51

Student B
You are Martin Clayton, Franchise Sales Director for Perfect Pizza.
Student A is interested in taking out a franchise with you.
Look at the following information and answer his or her questions.

Perfect Pizza
Perfect Pizza Ltd., Units 5 & 6, The Forum, Hanworth Lane, Chertsey, Surrey KT16 9JX. Tel. 0932 568000. Fax. 0921 570628.

Type of business: pizza delivery and takeaway
Applications invited: yes
Availability: all regions
Company established: 1978
Number of outlets in the UK: company owned 5, franchised 151
Working capital: £65,000
Liquid capital requirement: £25,000 – £30,000
Initial franchise fee: £8,000
On-going fees: management services fee 5%, marketing/advertising levy 3%
Typical outlet, projected turnover:
year 1 – £156,000, year 2 – £179,000, year 3 – £193,000
Typical outlet, projected profit:
year 1 – £25,000, year 2 – £32,600, year 3 – £36,500
Period of initial contract: 5 years
BFA membership: full

You should now play the role of a prospective franchisee who is interested in taking out a franchise with Budget Rent a Car. You have seen the advertisement opposite and decide to call Bernard Glover, Franchise Development Manager for Budget Rent a Car (played by Student A). Ask questions and complete the notes.
Examples: *How much liquid capital is required to set up an outlet?*
What is the initial franchise fee?

═ Budget ═

Budget Rent a Car is the world's largest franchised vehicle rental company with 3,500 locations worldwide.
With 160 offices each operating their own exclusive territory throughout the UK, we are looking to expand further.
To find out more about what makes *Budget Rent a Car* the natural choice in franchised

vehicle rental, please call Bernard Glover, our Franchise Development Manager, on 0442 218027.

Liquid capital requirement: ....
Working capital requirement: ....
Initial franchise fee: ....
On-going fees: ....
....
Projected turnover of typical outlet:
....
....
....
Projected profit of typical outlet:
....
....
....
Year company established: ....
Number of outlets: ....
Regions available: ....
Length of contract: ....

Unit 8, page 77

Student B

You are doing research for a retailer who is thinking of setting up a business specialising in the product that Student A has recently purchased. In order to obtain information both about local competition and about consumer buying habits, you must prepare a simple questionnaire. Your questionnaire should contain about 10–15 questions designed to find out the following information:

• Age, sex and occupation of the consumer
• Distance travelled to place of purchase

• Means of transport used to reach place of purchase
• Date and time of purchase
• Type of shop
• Amount of time spent in shop
• Reason for buying product
• Reason for choosing shop
• Means of payment
• Consumer satisfaction with product and shop

Example: *How old are you?*
What do you do for a living?

Unit 13, page 126

Student C

The graph opposite shows the EC's wheat exports for the period 1985-1990. Describe the information to your colleagues. Then listen to their descriptions and complete the graph for all four countries using the following key.

•—•—•—•—• Australia

———— USA

- - - - - - - - Canada

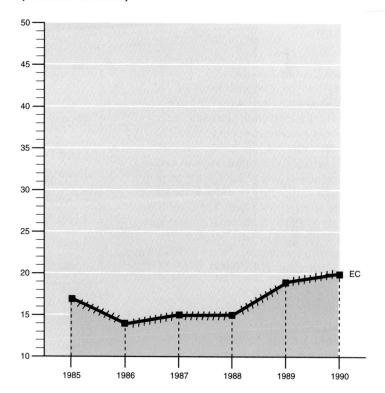

Wheat Exports 1985-1990
(in millions of tonnes)

Student B

You work for the Lombard Bank and have an appointment with a prospective client (Student A) who would like to deposit some money with your bank. The bank offers three different types of account, details of which are given below. Study this information and be prepared to answer Student A's questions and to give advice about which account(s) would best suit his or her saving requirements. In particular you should be ready to answer questions about the following:

• Minimum/Maximum opening deposits
• Interest rates
• Dates of interest payments
• Restrictions on withdrawing money

Notice Deposit Account

This account exists in three forms (3 months, 6 months and 14 days) depending on the period of notice. The rates of interest vary according to the notice period and interest payments can be made directly to the client or added to the sum in his or her notice deposit account to earn further interest. Additional deposits can be made without restriction.

Type of account	Deposit Min.	Max.	Interest rates per annum	Interest payments
Notice Deposit				
3 months	1000	–	8.75 (5.75*)	every 6 months
6 months	1000	–	9.0 (6.0*)	every 6 months
14 days	5000	–	9.25 (6.375*)	every 3 months

Note: *indicates interest rates payable when the balance is less than the minimum deposit.

Fixed Deposit Account

With this type of account funds are deposited for a fixed period of 1 to 5 years and earn interest at a fixed rate which is guaranteed not to change. The client can choose whether the interest is paid monthly, every three months, every six months or yearly. Interest can be paid directly to the client or added to the sum in the fixed term account. The client is not allowed to make withdrawals before the end of the fixed period of deposit. The minimum opening deposit is £1000 with a maximum limit of £250,000.

Type of account	Gross Rate % p.a. – interest paid annually		
	Amount of deposit		
	£1,000 – £24,999	£25,000 – £49,999	£50,000 – £250,000
Fixed Deposits			
1 year fixed period	9.00	9.125	9.25
2 year fixed period	9.00	9.125	9.25
3 year fixed period	9.25	9.375	9.50
4 year fixed period	9.25	9.375	9.50
5 year fixed period	9.25	9.375	9.50

Cheque Savings Account

This is an account for customers who want easy and instant access to their money while continuing to earn interest. Interest is paid every three months and customers are supplied with a chequebook which can be used without restriction. Customers may withdraw up to £1000 in cash per day but are not allowed to become overdrawn. Statements are sent every 6 months.

Type of account	
Cheque Savings Account	Interest paid
When the balance is £1,000 to £4,999	3.75
When the balance is £5,000 and above	6.00

Unit 11, page 103/104

Student C

SPECIFICATIONS	CAR A	CAR B	CAR C
Model			Lexus LS400
Price			£38,471
Type of engine			V8
Engine capacity			3,969 cc
Power			241 b.h.p.
Weight			1,802 kg.
Maximum speed			233 k.p.h.
Acceleration from 0-100 k.p.h.			8.6 secs
Petrol consumption (per 100 km) Town driving At 90 k.p.h.			14.4 l. 8.3 l.
Seating capacity			4
Additional information			Quietest car on the market, thick bumpers and strong front wings

Unit 13, page 126

Student D

The graph opposite shows Australia's wheat exports for the period 1985-1990. Describe the information to your colleagues. Then listen to their descriptions and complete the graph for all four countries using the following key.

——————— USA

- - - - - - - - Canada

⊦⊦⊦⊦⊦⊦ EC

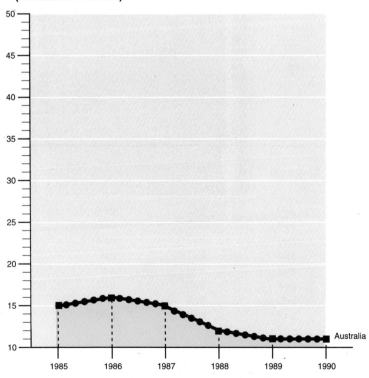

Wheat Exports 1985-1990
(in millions of tonnes)

151

Unit 2, page 23

Student B

You have been invited to attend an interview for a place on Renault's graduate management programme, as described in the advertisement on page 21. You will be interviewed by Sian Vernon (played by Student A), Personnel Officer for Renault UK Ltd. First give your CV and letter of application to Student A and then prepare for the interview. Think about the kind of questions that you are likely to be asked and plan your replies. Are there any questions that you would like to ask about the position?

Don't forget David Smyth's advice to interviewees (*Listening 1, page 22*).

Unit 10, page 96

High	Low	Stock	Price	Chng	Yld	P-E
CHEMICAL & PHARMACEUTICAL						
246	162	Alld Colloid	236	+6	2.2	18.7
682	413	Amersham	682	+2	2.4	25.3
774	583	BOC	743	+1	4.2	16.3
248	126	Blagden In	148	–	8.6	10.6
294	212	Brit Vita	259	+5	3.6	17.1
95	13	Caird Gp	26½	-0½	13.0	6.6
616	371	Courtaulds	546	+8	3.2	14.8
244	142	Croda	243	–	4.1	18.5
211	152	Ellis&Everard	186	-2	5.1	16.8
131	43	Evode	127	xd+1	3.8	–
403	143	Fisons	223	+1	5.2	16.2
943	632	Glaxo	717	+15	3.2	21.7
227	158	Hickson	200	-1	5.2	12.7
1410	975	ICI	1123	+26	6.5	27.1
660	434	Laporte	625	+2	4.0	16.8
328	138	Leigh Int	218	+4	4.8	17.8
290	11	MTM	13½	–	–	2.7
301	150	Medeva	211	–	.9	20.9
56	32	Ransom W	52	–	4.6	16.7
566	396½	SKBeechA	505	+9	2.0	20.5
503	353	SKBeechEU	445	+13	2.2	18.0
11	4½	Sutcliffe	10	–	–	–
1174	777	Wellcome	930	+17	1.9	25.7
397	253	Yorks Chems	393	-1	2.5	20.5
273	214	Yule Catto	266	–	2.7	16.2
FOOD MANUFACTURING						
178	75	Acatos&Hutch	174	–	5.1	9.8
83	31	Albert Fisher	69	–	7.2	11.5
515	362	Ass Brit Food	485	xd-9	3.8	11.1
147	103	Assoc Fish	137	–	6.8	25.3
181	109	Bibby (J)	124	–	11.1	6.9
490	312	Booker	422	+9	6.9	12.9
474	334	Brake Bros	450	-1	1.7	18.8
499	412	Cadbury-S	472	+4	3.5	17.4
107	64	Carrs Mill	83	–	6.3	16.6
435	275	Dalepak	310	–	2.6	13.9
487	352	Dalgety	482	–	5.4	16.0
54	27	Daniels S	30	–	1.1	32.8
440	249	Geest	374	–	2.8	14.2
470	375	Greggs	436	–	4.3	12.0
48	29½	Harrison M	42	–	5.7	–
180	81	Hazlewood	163	+7	5.0	9.9
200	68	Hillsdown	148	+2	7.9	8.9
61	27	Hunter Sap	42	+6	–	–
193	120	Linton Park	178	–	9.7	31.2
74	29	Matthews B	53	-1	–	11.2
317½	215	Nthn Foods	264	-3	4.0	14.5
223	78½	Park Foods	218	–	2.0	26.1
155	45	Perkins Fd	89	–	6.4	7.7
301	130	Ranks Hov	285	-5	6.5	14.6
443	285	Tate&Lyle	399	-3	4.0	14.7
368	192	Unigate	333	+3	6.1	11.9
440	222	Utd Bisc	355	+2	5.7	12.4
1000	575	Williamson T	600½	–	4.5	–

High	Low	Stock	Price	Chng	Yld	P-E
OIL & GAS						
186	115	Ampol	179	–	–	–
19½	11¼	Aran Egy	17¼	+0¼	–	–
53	27	Aus Oil&Gas	48	–	–	–
290	20	Aviva Pet	33	+1	–	–
304	182	BP	231	+0½	6.1	46.2
195	105	Br Borneo	159	–	6.0	17.5
295	223	Brit Gas	287	+1	6.2	13.2
4¼	1	Bula	1¼	–	–	–
741	460	Burmah Cstrol	683	–	4.7	15.6
75	21	Cairn Engy	39	–	–	–
246	164	Calor	229	–	7.0	15.1
80	20	Clyde	37	+2	–	70.2
467	297	Enterprise	411	+7	5.1	29.3
250	200	Flogas	215	–	4.9	8.4
69	34	Goal	48	+0½	3.5	9.1
31	5	Gt Western	25	+1	–	–
146	77	Hardy Oil	116	+1	1.1	36.4
6½	1½	KCA Drlling	2½	–	–	–
26½	7½	Kelt Enrgy	24	-1½	–	–
263	112	LASMO	146	–	7.8	18.9
40½	27	Monument	36¾	+0½	–	38.3
18½	5	New London	9½	–	–	–
37	25	Oil Search	27	–	–	–
48	8	Petrocon	9½	–	–	–
14	8	Petroz	12	–	–	–
31	10	Premier Cns	22¾	–	–	10.2
430	308	Ranger Oil	313	–	1.5	–
563	435	Shell	522	+4	5.3	21.0
82	26	Triton Eur	36	–	–	8.1
172	131	Woodside	149	+3½	2.4	–
TRANSPORT & SHIPPING						
440	211	A B Ports	360	–	3.0	77.1
816	531	BAA	788	+5	2.5	13.9
315	219	Br Airways	265	-2	5.1	7.1
182	45	Clarkson H	78	+1	–	3.5
101	11	Davies&New	23	–	–	–
488	293	Eurotunnel	396	+11	–	–
88	44	Fisher J	44	–	–	12.3
140	70	Graig Ship	138	–	4.4	–
39	22	Jacobs J	29	–	8.7	17.3
15¼	12¾	Manch Ship	12⅞	–	.5	5.2
311	190	Mersey Docks	299	-4	2.7	16.6
290	216	NFC	264	-3	3.3	19.9
153	54	Norex	149	-1	1.8	4.8
357	170	Ocean Group	283	+15	6.8	12.8
63	31	Ocean Wilson	40	–	8.9	8.9
555	296½	P&O	532	-1	7.6	18.8
156	97	P&O 5½%	130	–	5.6	–
1397	771	Seacon Hdgs	1270	+3	3.5	–
21	6½	Seafield	11	–	–	.9
59	23½	TIP Europe	24½	–	7.6	5.9
478	214	Tiphook	330	–	7.0	6.6
307	208	Trans Dev	277	–	4.6	16.6

Unit 12, page 114

Key			
1	a=0	b=2	c=4
2	a=4	b=2	c=0
3	a=0	b=2	c=4
4	a=4	b=2	c=0
5	a=2	b=4	c=0
6	a=4	b=0	c=2
7	a=0	b=4	c=2
8	a=2	b=4	c=0

Key			
9	a=2	b=4	c=0
10	a=0	b=2	c=4
11	a=0	b=4	c=2
12	a=2	b=4	c=0
13	a=2	b=0	c=4
14	a=2	b=4	c=0
15	a=0	b=4	c=2
16	a=4	b=2	c=0

Grammar Reference

PRESENT PERFECT AND PAST SIMPLE

Present perfect

■ We use the present perfect tense when there is a connection between the past and the present. It has two main uses:

a It is used when we are interested in the present result of something that happened at an unspecified time in the past:

*He's **decided** to look for a new job.*
*I'm afraid **I've forgotten** your name.*

b It is used to talk about an action or situation which started in the past and is still continuing:

*How long **have you worked** here?*
***She's been** away on business since last week.*
***I haven't seen** him for several years.*

■ Notice that we use *for* to show the duration of an action, and *since* to show when it began.

| *I've known her* | *for 3 months.* |
| | *since July.* |

■ The present perfect is often used with adverbs such as *just, yet, still, already, ever, never, recently, lately, so far, up to now.*

*They've **just** signed an important contract.*
*She hasn't received an answer **yet**.*
*Have you **ever** used this type of machine?*
*We've had good results **so far**.*

Past simple

We use the past simple tense to talk about something which happened in the past and which has no connection with the present. It refers to a finished period of time:

*Pasteur **made** important medical discoveries.*

***Did** you **go** to the meeting yesterday?*
*She **worked** in Paris for five years before moving to Rome.*

PRESENT SIMPLE AND PRESENT CONTINUOUS

Present simple

We use the present simple to talk about habitual actions, and things which are generally true.

*She **usually stays** at the Hilton, but it was fully booked.*
*Metals **expand** when heated.*

Present continuous

■ We use the present continuous to talk about something which is happening at or around the time of speaking.

*Angela's in London **at the moment. She's staying** at the Hotel Intercontinental.*
***We're expanding** our operations in the Far East.*

■ We use the present continuous to talk about temporary situations, and the present simple to talk about permanent situations.

***I'm working** in a bookshop **during the summer holidays**.*
*He **works** in the Personnel Department of a large multinational company.*

■ Certain verbs are **not** normally used in the continuous form. For example, we say *I know* (not *~~I am knowing~~*) and *I like* (not *~~I am liking~~*). Common verbs of this type include:

Verbs of feeling	
like	dislike
love	hate
want	appreciate
prefer	

Verbs of thinking		
know	understand	think
believe	forget	remember
recognise	realise	mean

Verbs of senses	
see	feel
hear	smell
taste	

Other verbs	
belong	have (= possess)
own	contain
consist of	include
be	exist

PRESENT TENSES WITH A FUTURE MEANING

Present simple

We use the present simple for the future when referring to timetables or programmes.

*The meeting **starts** at 3 o'clock.*
*Our flight **arrives** at 6 p.m.*

Present continuous

We use the present continuous to talk about future arrangements and plans.

*I'm **attending** a meeting tomorrow afternoon.*
*We're **flying** to Hamburg next week.*

GERUND AND INFINITIVE

Gerund (verb + *ing*)

■ In English, several verbs are followed by the gerund. Some of these verbs are given in the following list:

admit	imagine
appreciate	involve
avoid	postpone
consider	propose
delay	risk
enjoy	stop
finish	suggest

*The department head **proposed organising** a meeting for all staff members.*
*This job **involves analysing** our sales figures since 1989.*

■ The gerund can be the subject of a sentence:

*In the US, **getting** into commercials is often a sign a career is on the way down.*
***Developing** new products will be our main objective next year.*

■ The gerund must be used immediately after prepositions, for example:

after	when
before	while
by	without

*They launched the product **without doing** the necessary research.*

It must also be used after verbs and expressions followed by prepositions, for example:

to be interested in	to think of/about
to be good at	to look forward to
to be fond of	to succeed in
to be for/against	to approve of
to be used to	to insist on
instead of	to object to
to feel like	

*I **am used to travelling** abroad.*
*We're **looking forward to meeting** the new sales manager.*

■ Note that we also use the gerund after the following expressions:

it's no use	it's not worth
it's no good	to have difficulty

*It's **no use trying** to phone him. He's on holiday.*

Infinitive

■ In English, several verbs are followed by the infinitive. Some of these verbs are given in the following list:

afford	hope	refuse
agree	learn	seem
choose	manage	tend
decide	offer	threaten
forget	plan	
help	promise	

*Agents for several movie stars **refused to comment.***
*I **hope to find** a job in marketing.*

■ The infinitive is used after modals, either with or without *to*:

Verb + infinitive with *to*		
have to	ought to	used to

Verb + infinitive without *to*		
can	might	should
could	must	will
may	shall	would

*We **used to sell** only computers, but we now sell most types of electronic equipment.*
*You **should send** these letters by fax by the end of the day.*

Gerund or infinitive?

■ Some verbs can be followed by either a gerund or infinitive, for example:

begin	like	stop
can't bear	love	try
continue	remember	
hate	start	

*Our star **hates to be mentioned**.*
*I **hate working** long hours.*

■ Some of these verbs have different meanings depending on whether they are used with the gerund or the infinitive.

to remember + gerund = to remember something done in the past
to remember + infinitive = not to forget to do something

*I **remember seeing** that advertisement in the newspaper last week.*
*I must **remember to cancel** the order before one o'clock.*

to try + gerund = to do something as an experiment, for example to see if it is successful or enjoyable
to try + infinitive = to make an attempt to do something

***Try asking** Sally. She may be able to help you.*
*I **tried not to laugh**.*

RELATIVE CLAUSES

Defining relative clauses

■ The following relative pronouns can be used to introduce a defining relative clause:

	to refer to people	to refer to things
Subject	who, that	which, that
Object	(who, that, whom*)	(which, that)
Possessive	whose	

*Note that whom is mainly used in formal, written English.

■ When *that, who* or *which* are the object of the verb in the relative clause, they can be omitted.

■ Commas are not used to separate the relative clause from the rest of the sentence.

*Some of the applicants (**who/that**) we interviewed were very highly qualified.*
*The job (**that/which**) they asked us to do was almost impossible.*

Non-defining relative clauses

■ The following relative pronouns can be used to introduce a non-defining relative clause:

	to refer to people	to refer to things
Subject	who	which
Object	who, whom	which
Possessive	whose	

■ *That* cannot be used in a non-defining clause.

■ *Who* or *which* cannot be omitted.

■ Commas are usually used to separate the relative clause from the rest of the sentence.

*The manager, **who was in his late fifties**, accepted early retirement.*

EXPRESSING CONTRAST

■ There are several ways of expressing contrast in English:

a

although even though though	+ subject + verb

*He enjoys his job, **although** he would like more responsibility.*
__Even though__ she works long hours, she still finds time for other things.
*She's never been to Japan, **though** she's fluent in Japanese.*

b

despite in spite of	+ noun or + verb + ing

__Despite__ the recession, we achieved record profits.
*They still think they'll win the election, **in spite of** the recent opinion polls.*
*I haven't finished that report yet, **despite** working overtime last night.*

We can also say *despite the fact that …* or *in spite of the fact that …* .
__Despite__ the fact that I worked overtime last night, I haven't finished that report.

■ Compare the following sentences which have the same meaning:

__Although__ sales fell sharply last month, we are on target for the year.
__Despite__ the sharp fall in sales last month, we are on target for the year.

THE PASSIVE

■ Compare the following sentences:

Active: *Anita Roddick* **opened** *the first branch of The Body Shop in 1976.*
Passive: *The first branch of The Body Shop* **was opened** *in 1976.*

The two sentences have the same meaning, but the emphasis is different:

In an active sentence, we are more interested in the person or thing doing the action (the agent).
In a passive sentence, we are more interested in the person or thing affected by the action. If we want to mention the agent, we use *by*:

The first branch of The Body Shop **was opened by** *Anita Roddick in 1976.*

But often the agent is not important:

Our products **are made** *entirely of recycled materials.*
Maria **has been** *promoted.*

■ There are passive forms of most verb tenses, for example:

Present simple	*Every item* **is checked** *for quality.*
Present continuous	*Whole forests* **are being destroyed**.
Present perfect	*Nothing* **has been touched** *since you left.*
Past simple	*The company* **was founded** *in 1903.*
Past continuous	*The machinery* **wasn't being used** *efficiently.*
Past perfect	*A decision* **had** *already* **been reached**.

■ After *will, can, may, must, should, could, ought to* etc. we use *be* + the past participle.

The designs **will be finished** *by the end of the week.*
The new computer **should be delivered** *on Friday.*

MAKE AND DO

■ We use *do* when we talk about an activity without mentioning exactly what it is.

What's she **doing**?
Are you **doing** *anything tonight?*

■ *Do* is often used when we talk about work or a task. It is also used in the structure *do + -ing*.

Have you **done** *your homework yet?*
It was a pleasure **doing** *business with you.*
Could you **do** *some photocopying for me, please?*

■ *Make* often has the meaning of 'create' or 'construct'.

We **made** *a new design for the product based on his suggestions.*
The company **makes** *photographic equipment.*

■ *Make* is often used with nouns connected with talking and sounds:

make *a complaint, an enquiry, a noise, a remark*
and travelling:
make *a journey, a visit*

■ There are however, many other expressions which do not follow these guidelines and it is best to learn these or use a dictionary if you are unsure. For example:

do: *good, your best, harm, someone a favour*
make: *an appointment, arrangements, an attempt, a choice, money, progress, a start*

FIRST, SECOND AND THIRD CONDITIONAL

First conditional

We use the first conditional to talk about the consequences of something which may possibly happen in the future.

If *you* **transfer** *your money to a deposit account,* **you'll earn** *more interest.*
I'll give *you a five per cent discount* **if** *you* **pay** *by cash.*

Note that we use a present tense in the *if*-clause, and a future tense in the main clause.

Second conditional

■ We use the second conditional to talk about something which we think is unlikely to happen, or to refer to an imaginary situation.

What **would** *you* **do if** *you* **lost** *your credit card?*
If *I* **had** *more money,* **I'd invest** *it on the Stock Exchange.*

Note that we use a past tense in the *if*-clause, and *would* + infinitive in the main clause.

■ When the verb *to be* is used in the *if*-clause, we sometimes use *were* instead of *was*, especially after *I*.

If **I weren't** *so tired, I would gladly help you.*

■ We often use the expression *If I were you* for giving someone advice.

If I were you, *I would take traveller's cheques rather than cash.*

Third conditional

We use the third conditional to talk about actions or events which did not happen in the past, but which could have happened.

If *you* **had bought** *shares in Norcros, you* **would have made** *a lot of money.*

The employees **would not have gone** *on strike* **if** *the company* **had improved** *their pension schemes.*

Note that we use the past perfect tense in the *if*-clause, and *would have* + past participle in the main clause.

REPORTED SPEECH

When we want to relate what someone said or thought, we can either use direct speech or reported speech. There are several changes that take place when converting direct speech into reported speech. Look at the following example:

Direct speech: *'We are totally committed to product quality,'* *said Paul Moore.*
Reported speech: *Paul Moore said that they were totally committed to product quality.*

Note that the present tense verb in direct speech (*are*) becomes a past tense verb in reported speech (*were*). Such tense changes take place when the reporting verb (e.g. *said, told, asked*) is in the past. Other tense changes can be summarised as follows:

Direct speech	Reported speech
Present simple ⟶	Past simple
Present continuous ⟶	Past continuous
Past simple ⟶	Past perfect
Present perfect ⟶	Past perfect
Past perfect ⟶	Past perfect
will ⟶	would
can ⟶	could

MODAL VERBS: OBLIGATION

■ The following modal verbs can be used to express varying degrees of obligation.

Obligation or necessity	Mild obligation or advice	Absence of obligation or necessity
have to must/mustn't need to	should/shouldn't ought to	don't have to don't need to

■ Note that there is sometimes a difference between *must* and *have to*. *Must* is used to talk about what we personally consider to be important. *Have to* is used to talk about an obligation that is imposed from outside.

I must finish this today. (I would like to start working on the new project tomorrow.)
I have to attend a meeting. (The boss has asked me to attend a meeting.)

■ Note also that the negative forms of *must* and *have to* have two very different meanings. We use *mustn't* to indicate that it is important not to do something, for example because it is forbidden. We use *don't have to* to indicate that there is no obligation to do something – you can do it if you want to, but it is not necessary.

You mustn't tell her. (Don't tell her.)
You don't have to tell her. (You can tell her if you want to, but it isn't necessary.)

THE ARTICLE

The indefinite article (*a/an*)

We use the indefinite article (*a/an*):

■ when we refer to a singular countable noun for the first time.

I've just been given a new company car.
Could you book me a hotel for next week?

■ with jobs and nouns of nationality. Unlike in some languages, the article **cannot** be omitted.

She's an accountant.
She's an American and her husband is a Scotsman.

The definite article (*the*)

We use the definite article (*the*):

■ when we already know what is being talked about, or when we are referring to a specific person or thing.

The car cost nearly £40,000.
What's the name of the hotel we're staying in?

■ when the noun referred to is the only one of its kind, for example *the sun, the world, the Queen*.

■ when we use an adjective as a noun to refer to a group of people, for example *the rich, the old, the unemployed, the homeless, the British, the Spanish.*

■ in superlative constructions, for example *the fastest, the most expensive, the best, the worst.*

No article

We do not use an article:

■ with plural and uncountable nouns when making general statements.

Cars are a major cause of pollution.
Gas is cheaper than electricity.

■ with certain types of nouns, such as school subjects, meals and abstract nouns.

I'm studying chemistry.
What did you have for breakfast?
Loyalty to one's company is very common in Japan.

■ in certain prepositional phrases, for example *at home, at university, in bed, by train, at night.*

Word List

A

account, p.78
account (for), p.6, 44
account, (to take something into …), p.26
accountant, p.4
achieve, p.8, 46
acquisition, p.98
add, p.65, 102
administrative, p.14
advertise, p.38, 101
advertising, p.34
advertising agency, p.38
afford, p.36
agency, p.19
agenda, p.32
agreement, p.45, 49
aim, p.45
alliance, p.99
allowance, p.14
analyst, p.54
annual earnings, p.32
annual report, p.86
apply, p.14
appointments page, p.14
asset, p.138
attend, p.47
authority, p.24, 55
average, p.6, 50

B

back up, p.51, 63, 71
background, p.24
balance, p.82
balance sheet, p.84
bank note, p.79
bank statement, p.79
benefits, p.5
bill, p.79
Board of Directors, p.4
bond, p.88
bonus, p.27
boom, p.46
borrow, p.44
brand, p.11, 41, 63, 78, 109, 138
break-even, p.52
bribe, p.84
brochure, p.63
broker, p.91, 130
budget, p.7
business connections, p.101
business consultancy, p.31
business plan, p.115

C

campaign, p.38, 62
candidate, p.14
capital, p.91, 99, 109
career, p.14
carry out, p.138
case study, p.32, 67
cash machine, p.79
chain, p.45
chain store, p.69
Chairperson, p.4
Chamber of Commerce, p.19
charge, p.80
charge, (to be in … of), p.8, 10
chartered accountants, p.14
cheque, p.82,
chequebook, p.79
Chief Executive Officer, p.4
City (the), p.131
claim, (noun, vb), p.131
clause, p.37
clearing bank, p.78
client, p.32, 37, 130
cohesive, p.138
coin, p.79
colleague, p.48
come up with, p.8
commercial bank, p.78
commission, p.91
commitment, p.86, 138
communicative ability, p.23
company secretary, p.106
compensation, p.55, 128
competitive, p.14, 98
components, p.105
computer assisted technology, p.14
confirm, p.100
consultant, p.47, 59
consumer, p.4, 6, 67
contract, p.43, 100
contribute, p.17
corporate identity, p.136
corporate partnership, p.99
cost, p.43
counterpart, p.26, 90, 118
covering letter, p.14
credit, p.82
credit card, p.79
credit rating, p.86
currency, p.121
current account, p.78
curriculum vitae, p.14
customer, p.41, 71
customer services, p.14, 73
cut-price, p.71

D

deal, p.72, 118
deal (with), p.50
dealer, p.103
debit, p.82
debit card, p.79
decrease, p10
degree (university), p.14, 24
delegation, p.32
deliver, p.108
demonstration, p.63, 81
department store, p.36, 69
deposit, (vb), p.82, 96
designed for, (to be), p.41
direct mail, p.34
discontinue, p.65
discount, p.72
distribute, p.101
distribution system, p.31, 72
dividend, p.88, 133
documentary, p.65
duty, p.116, 119
duty free, p.100

E

earn, p.99
economies of scale, p.99
effectively, p.100
efficient, p.49
employee, p.16
employer, p.16
enclosed, p.19
endorse, p.35
endorsement, p.35
engineer, p.4
enterprise, p.26
entrepreneur, p.109
environment, p.61
environmentally friendly, p.67
equal-opportunity, p.16
equity, p.88
establish, p.47, 100
estimate, p.32
executive, p.24, 36
exhibition, p.17, 47
expansion, p.47
expenses, p.72
experience, p.14
expertise, p.46, 82
exploit, p.17
export, (noun, vb), p.6, 116
exporter, p.118
extract, (vb), p.65

F

factory, p.4, 63
failure, p.52

fax, p.119
fee, p.37, 43
finance, p.4
financial incentives, p.26
financier, p.111
flexible, (to be), p.31
flow chart, p.23
foothold, p.45, 99
forecast, p.31, 45, 47
foreign currency, p.86
found, p.9
founder, p.71
franchise agreement, p.43
franchisee, p.43
franchisor, p.43
free of charge, p.82
freight, p.120
fund-raising, p.62
funds, p.82

G

generate, p.63
gilt-edged security, p.88
global market, p.100
global warming, p.67
goal, p.8
goods, p.44, 120
government stock, p.88
graduate, p.24, 56
grow, p.9, 47

H

head, (vb), p.10
headhunter, p.17
headline, p.55
headquarters, p.8, 14
health insurance, p.14
hierarchy, p.24
highlight, (vb), p.19
hire, p.16
human resources, p.4
hypermarket, p.69

I

impact, p.138
import, (noun, verb), p.116
improve, p.67
impulse, p.77
income, p.40, 77
increase, (vb), p.7, 10
information technology, p.105
initiative, p.24
innovate, p.7
inquiry, p.4
intended for, (to be), p.41
inter-personal skills, p.14

interest, p.82, 109
interest (to take an … in), p.24
interview, p.14
invest, p.101
investment, p.9, 80, 92
invoice, p.82, 120
involved, (to be), p.19
issue, (vb), p.61, 86, 88
item, p.76

J

jobber, p.90
joint venture, p.26, 45, 98

K

keyboard, p.79

L

label, (vb), p.65, 73
labour, p.51, 119
launch, (noun, vb), p.8, 63
layout, p.76
lead, (vb), p.24
leadership, p.23, 51
leaflet, p.34, 73
lease, p.109
letter of application, p.14
liaison, p.119
licence, (vb), p.46, 100
life assurance, p.90
life insurance, p.131
lifestyle, p.39, 40
liquid capital, p.51
listed company, p.89
loan, p.78, 88, 109
local partner, p.31
location, p.47
logo, p.136
losses, p.62

M

machinery, p.108
management, p.4
management consultant, p.32
Managing Director, p.4, 63
manufacturing, p.5
margin, p.70
market, (noun, vb), p.40, 50
market leader, p.99
market research, p.31
marketing, p.4, 34
marketing mix, p.34, 35
mass market, p.72
master licence, p.45
meant for, (to be), p.41
meeting, p.26
membership, p.52, 92
memorandum, p.58
merchant bank, p.78
merger, p.98
microchip, p.104
mobilize, p.62
model, p.71, 72
monetary policy, p.78
monitor, (vb), p.16
mortgage, p.110
multinational, p.5
multiple retailer, p.69

N

negotiate, p.47, 59, 99
negotiation, p.31, 60
network, p.39, 99
niche, p.71
non-contributory pension, p.14
non-profit-making organisation,
  p.19

O

objective, p.33, 100
open-minded, (to be), p.31
operate, p.47, 100
operator, p.47
order, p.17, 72, 109
ordinary share, p.88
organisation chart, p.4
outlet, p.46, 69
output, p.55
overdraft, p.87
overdraw, p.87
overheads, p.72, 108
overseas, p.14
overtime, p.55
owe, p.53
own, p.47
ownership, p.97

P

packaging, p.9, 34, 67
pan-European, p.99
partner, p.27
partnership, p.9, 45, 92, 106
patent, p.7
pay (attention to), p.24
payment, p.51, 82
pension scheme, p.90
performance, p.7, 31
personnel, p.4, 14
plummet, (vb), p.37
point out, p.62, 100
policy, p.8, 70, 128
poll, p.55, 138
pollution, p.67
predict, p.47, 100
premises, p.109
premium, p.128
prerequisite, p.6
pricing, p.34, 70
private limited company, p.106
procedure, p.14
produce, (noun, vb), p.65, 118
product, p.63
production, p.4, 55
professional experience, p.19
profile, p.17, 27
profit, p.72, 106
programme, p.63, 81
project an image, p.136
promote, p.16, 37, 70
promotion, p.17, 34
property, p.109
protectionist, p.116
public limited company, p.106
public relations, p.4, 19, 63
publicity, p.36, 62, 70
publicize, p.63
purchase, (noun, vb), p.73, 82,
  96, 98

Q

quality, p.14, 105
quota, p.116
quote, (vb), p.91

R

raise, (vb), p.62
range, p.50, 72
rank, (vb), p.16, 47
rate, p.44
rationalise, p.27
reach an agreement, p.102
reach objectives, p.24
ready cash, p.51
receipt, p.72, 79
recruit, (vb), p.14
recruitment technique, p.16
recyclable, p.9, 68
redundancies, p.26
redundant (make sb.), p.26
references, p.19
regulation, p.119
re-insurance, p.129, 130
relocation, p.14
remove, p.65
repayment, p.108
report, (noun, vb), p.10, 17, 48
research and development, p.4, 98
research, p.7, 26, 76
resources, p.100
responsibility, p.14, 61
responsible for, (to be), p.10, 14,
  138
restrict, p.127
retailer, p.45, 63, 72
retailing, p.69
return, (noun, vb), p.46, 65
risk, p.128
rival, p.46
rule, p.27, 44
run, (vb), p.8, 37
run a campaign, p.136

S

sack, (vb), p.26
salary, p.5
sales, p.13, 98
sales assistant, p.19, 73
savings, p.92
savings account, p.84
scheme, p.108
screen, p.79
sector, p.8, 21
secure, p.72
security, p.91
self-starters, p.50
seminar, p.59
senior manager, p.4
set up, (vb), p.8, 63, 109
share, p.88
shareholder, p.4, 71, 88, 106
shift, p.55
shipment, p.120
shortlist, p.14
skills, p.14, 24
slogan, p.35, 37
society, p.129, 130
software, p.17, 48
sole proprietor, p.106
sole trader, p.106

specialisation, p.17
spokesman/spokeswoman, p.37, 45
sponsor, (noun, vb), p.9, 143
staff, p.8
stake, p.88, 105
stand for, p.138
statements, p.61
status symbol, p.37
stock, p.51, 72, 99
strategy, p.8, 63
stress, (vb), p.100
strike, (to go on), p.49
subscribe to, p.90
subsidiary, p.8, 98
subsidy, p.127
succeed, p.47
suit, (vb), p.27
sum, p.43
superstore, p.69
supplier, p.27, 72
supplies, p.44
surplus, p.72, 127
survey, p.24, 44, 55, 56
survive, p.100
syndicate, p.131

T

takeover, p.98
target audience, p.34
target, p.40
tariff, p.116
tax holiday, p.100
team spirit, p.23
telecommunications, p.105
tend, (vb), p.50
theft, p.128
third party, p.128
topic, p.32, 65
track record, p.21, 51
trade, (noun, vb), p.7, 63, 88
trade barriers, p.45
trade fair, p.17
trade union, p.91
train, (vb), p.6, 24
trainees, p.65
training course, p.17
training programmes, p.14
transaction, p.82, 91
traveller's cheques, p.79
trend, p.70, 86
turnover, p.13, 72, 97, 101

U

underwrite, p.128
unemployment, p.127
update, (vb), p.91, 142
upscale image, p.99

V

value, p.135

W

warehouse, p.72
wealth, p.134
wholesale, p.90
withdraw, p.83
word-processing, p.14
workforce, p.4
working capital, p.51
worth, p.119

Addison Wesley Longman Limited
Edinburgh Gate, Harlow,
Essex CM20 2JE, England
and Associated Companies throughout the world.

This edition published by
Addison Wesley Longman Ltd, 1996

ISBN 0-17-556883-9

Fifth impression 1997

Printed in China
GCC/05

Acknowledgements

The authors would like to thank the
following for their help: Ben Marsh, Linda
Kehr Grams, Jill A Berke, 3M plc, St Paul
MN; Pip Frankish,3M UK plc and Hervé
Naux of 3M France; Peter Iwarson, MoDo;
Gerald Adams, Utah State University;
Joanna Lawrence, ICI; Nathalie Baudoin,
Patagonia GMBH; Norman A. Jacobs,
Eastpak, Inc.; Meda Stamper, The Coca
Cola Company; John L. Henry, Uniglobe
Travel (International) Inc.; American
Management Association, New York; Polly
Platt; Intercultural Management Associates;
Business Principles London; Ancient
Recipes; Dan Cassidy, Glasgow
Polytechnic; Association of British Insurers;
David Brodala, Perfect Pizza; The City
Business Library, London; INSEAD
Library, Fontainebleau, France; Peter J.
Griffiths, Reuters, London; International
Management; The Manager and Staff of the
Longacre Body Shop, London; Phil Talbot,
Pascale du Verne and Tracey Pearce of The
Body Shop; Rhys Davis of Business; James
Johnson-Flint, Richer Sounds plc; Dr Leigh
Sparks, Stirling University Institute for
Retail Studies; Maureen Cork, Banking
Information Service, London; Caroline
Paylor, Colin Mayes, London Stock
Exchange; Anne Blisset, Jeanette Newman,
Ivor Googe, Corporate Communications,
BP plc; British Franchising Association;
Renault, France Ltd.

The publishers would like to thank the
following for their kind permission to use
their material in this book:

Eurobusiness for 3M: An American Star in
Europe by Tim Hindle, p.6; Colgate
Palmolive, p.9; MoDo, p.12; Virgin France,
p.146; *International Herald Tribune*, Looks:
Appearance Counts With Many Managers
by Sherry Buchanan, p.16; Patagonia
GMBH, Munich, p.18; Renault UK Ltd,
p.21; *The European*, Be nice and smile if
you want to hire a Hungarian manager,
Steve Lodge; *The Washington Post*, In Ads,
US Stars Shine For Japanese Eyes Only by
Margaret Shapiro, p.36; The Coca-Cola
Company, Atlanta, p.39; *The European*,
Small Slice of the Big Action by Iain
McKilvie, p.45; Benetton Public Relations,
France, p.48; Uniglobe Travel
(International) Inc., p.47; Perfect Pizza, UK,
p.51; Budget Rent a Car International Inc.,
UK, p.51-2, 148; *US News and World
Report*, Dying to Work by Jim Impoco, p.54;
Cartoonists and Writers Syndicate, p.61;
World Press Review, p.61; *Inc.*, A Banner of
Values, by Bo Burlingham, p.63; The Body
Shop, p.51-68; The Proctor and Gamble
Company, p.67; *Business*, Richer Pickings
by Nigel Cope, p.71; Richer Sounds plc,
p.73; Marks and Spencer, p.73; Bank of
Scotland, Hobs, p.80; Lombard Bank, p.150;
Banking Information Service, London, The
Stock Exchange, p.90; *The Independent*,
p.94, 152; Thorntons p.92; *Time*, Getting
together by Michael S. Serrill, p.99;
Motokov, p.101; Renault, p.147; *Financial
Times*, Deliver us from debt by Nicholas
Garnett, p.108; *Super Marketing*, The
Spanish Oracle by Keely Harrison, p.118;
British Invisibles Corporation of London,
Insurance Services p.129; Prudential
Corporation plc., London, p.132; BP plc,
p.137, 139; Perrier p.141.

The authors would also like to thank the
following people for their co-operation in
allowing us to interview them: Manley
Johnson, 3M France, p.10, 11; David Smyth,
Europe Assistance, p.22; Tom Scheck,
Profile, p.31; Manfred Kozlowsky, Harley-
Davidson GMH, p.41; John P. Hayes, The
Hayes Group Inc., p.50; Kay Ainsley,
Domino's Pizza, p.50; Klaus G. Ueber,
Natural Beauty Products Ltd, p.50; Tony
Datfield, British Franchise Association,
p.44; Tomomi Moriwake, p.59; David
Wheeler, Body Shop, p.68; Dr Steve Burt,
Stirling University Institute for Retail
Studies, p.70; Peter Milson, Midland Bank,
p.78; Alain Depussé, p.86; Stuart Valentine,
The London Stock Exchange, p.97;
Margareta Galfard, Volvo, France, p.105;
Ben Fox, Fasta Pasta, p.107, 113; OECD,
Paris, p.116, 127; Glen Tuttsell, Michael
Peters Ltd, p.142.

Photographs
ATS, p.142; The Bank of Scotland, p.80;
British Broadcasting Corporation, p.142;
Benetton Public Relations, France, p.48;
BMW, p.103; The Body Shop International
plc, p.62-5, 68; Stuart Boreham
Photography, p.18; BP plc, p.137, 139-41;
Budget Rent a Car, p.52; J. Allan Cash
Photo Library, p.77; The Coca Cola
Company, p.34; Eastpak Inc., p.40; Fiat,
p.104; The Financial Times/ Tony Andrews,
p.108; Harley-Davidson, p.41; Harrods Ltd,
p.69; IBM, p.34; Kentucky Fried Chicken,
p.43; Kwik Fit, p.43; Lexus Cars, p.104;
Mars Confectionery, p.34; The Midland
Bank, p.78; Modo, p.12; The Image Bank,
p.32; Perfect Pizza, p.51; Perrier, p.141;
Philips, p.31; Reed Business Publications,
p.118; Keith Reed, p.19, 45, 69, 71, 111;
Renault Cars, p.104-105; Rex Features p.36,
99, 130; Chris Ridgers Photography, p.9, 34,
77; Marcus Robinson, p.129; The Science
Photo Library p.67; The Telegraph Colour
Library, p.117; Tesco Creative Services,
p.69; Thorntons Confectionery, p.92; Tony
Stone Worldwide, p.11, 16, 54, 56, 77, 78;
3M, p.5-8; Vauxhall Cars, p.112; Walkers
Shortbread Ltd, p.40.

Illustrated by Helen E. Porter.